The Miracle
OF THE
MUNDANE
Falling in Love with Living

Mark Carnes

The Miracle of the Mundane
ISBN: 979-8-218-47531-4
©Copyright 2024 by Mark Carnes

Shawhine
PUBLICATIONS

Scripture quotations taken from: New Living Translation (NLT) Copyright © 2000 by Tyndale House Publishers; New International Version (NIV) Copyright © 1984 by Zondervan; English Standard Version (ESV) © Bible Gateway; New King James Version (NKJV) © Bible Gateway.

Contents

In Conclusion

Introduction

This is a book written for helping people to fall in love with every single moment of living life. At least, that was my motivation when compiling it. Whether or not it does that, I cannot guarantee. My hope and prayer is that in some way, shape, or form, it will help you look at life through a lens that helps you discover a passionate appreciation for life, and a longing hope for eternal life beyond this temporary existence on planet earth.

I'm not sure I can classify it as a self-help book. I'm really not sure I can classify it as any type of book in particular. I am not much of an expert at anything other than my own life experiences and how I have processed them through my world-view and personal reflections and reactions. Perhaps in that sense, it is simply a book that reflects my way of looking at and walking through both the simple and profound things of life.

In writing this book, I had a motivation for inspiring and encouraging people from all walks and stages of life. If I'm honest, the writing of this book was also very therapeutic for me. It helped me to process many of the events of my life in a more robust and life-affirming way.

This book is a compilation of a few of my own personal life experiences and reflections. There are many of my life stories and experiences left untold, and not in this book. Perhaps I will tell those in a follow-up book. These are not necessarily the best or most profound stories, or even the ones I saved up for the book. They are just the ones I chose to write about.

This book is not an attempt to get anyone to think the way I do about living. Not everyone will have had my life experiences or even see things through my world-view. Maybe it's best that way. Maybe all you will learn is something more about me, if you're even interested. But maybe (and this is my prayer), just maybe it will spark something in you that you have lost or did not know was even there. Maybe it will encourage you. Maybe it will make you cry. Maybe it will make you relate. Maybe it will make you question. Maybe it will challenge you. Maybe it will give you the desire to process something differently or to try again. Maybe it will make you love more fully or extend grace and forgiveness where it is needed—maybe even to yourself. Or maybe it will just make you smile. If any of this happens, perhaps that was my goal in writing the book.

There is a "Contents" page, and the stories are separated into different chapters and sections. However, there is no particular order in which they must be read. Some personal stories are seasonal, while some are dealing with other stages of life. They can all be read in order, or you can start from anywhere in the book. Hopefully, you will be encouraged to read them again and again, particularly when you need them.

I have learned in this life that little things are not little. I have learned that there are sights and sounds beneath the sights and sounds. There is so much more in life to be experienced than we typically allow ourselves to experience, in both the good and the hard. There are tears to be shed, more smiles to be had, more moments to grab hold of and ponder, and there are miracles in the mundane of our routine experience. Most of all, I believe that all these things are preparing and pointing us to something that is greater than the sum of all of them—eternity in Heaven.

The God who created us is not random. He has a divine, extraordinary plan and purpose for every moment of our lives, particularly when we surrender them to His will. All of those things point us to the ultimate destination—glory! Perhaps that's too trite for some. But for me, it is the reason for everything. I have built my life upon it and it is the reason for my way of looking at things. Whether you agree or not, perhaps you will at least find value and purpose in your own journey. Perhaps you will find the miraculous in your own mundane experience. Perhaps that will point you to being able to see the extraordinary in the ordinary. Or maybe, just maybe you will find a touch of glory through something that is way bigger than you. It all matters, and it is all extraordinarily miraculous!

Life, Time, and Moments

1
Abundant Life

Jesus said in John 10:10 (NIV), "The thief comes only to steal, kill, and destroy; but I come that they may have life, and have it to the full." The immediate implication here is eternal life. It is the ultimate question. Have you trusted Christ as your Lord and Savior and received the full and eternal life He gives? There is no life apart from Him. There is a real Enemy, Satan, who is hell-bent on keeping you from that life. But if Satan can't keep you from that life, he'll still do everything he can to keep you from the fullness of that life.

Perhaps you have trusted Christ as your Savior. But is the fullness of His resurrection life alive in you? Is Jesus fully Himself in and through You? This is His desire for us! While the Enemy cannot take our assurance of salvation, he will still try to "steal, kill, and destroy" the joy and fullness of our life in Christ. He will make every attempt to render us ineffective for Christ and steal our enjoyment in Christ. He will try to make serving Christ more laborious rather than the joy for which Christ intended it.

On the day of Jesus' resurrection, Luke 24:1-2, 5-6 tells us, "Very early on Sunday morning the women went to the tomb, taking the spices they had prepared. They found that the stone had been rolled away from the entrance. The angel said, 'Why are you looking for the living among the dead? He is not here! He is risen from the dead, just as He said."

As far as the disciples were concerned, it was just another day. The sun came up the same as it usually does. It was just another day in the life of the routine. Sadly, their routine now included grief and mourning. But something was about to break into their routine that would change their lives forever.

Perhaps they still held out hope that Jesus would rise from the dead as He said He would. But recent events did not give them cause for much hope. For the two Mary's, as far as we know in the text, they were simply coming to look at the tomb. They were coming to anoint and pay their respects to Jesus. They had very little expectation of an encounter with a resurrected Jesus. They had very little expectation that their lives were about to be lifted into the extraordinary...right there in their ordinary.

We can tend to be just like the two Mary's that day. We've walked with Jesus, we've talked with Jesus, we've encountered Jesus. But if we're honest, much of the time, we have no resurrection expectations of Jesus on a daily basis. We rise to the mundane of each day. The sun comes up the same as it did yesterday. We race off to the routine. We may take a moment to look at Jesus. We may take a moment to pay our respects to Jesus. But we have no real expectations of an encounter with the resurrected Jesus in the mundane of our day to day routine.

The angel made the pronouncement that day, "Why are you looking for the living among the dead? He is not here! He is risen!" The world in which we live is filled with dead places. But if you have trusted Christ Jesus as Lord, you are not among the dead. Your dead places have been brought to life! In every crevice, in every crack, and in every unnoticed moment of your routine, daily life, there are miraculous, resurrection moments waiting to lift you above the ordinary, and change you forever.

For the disciples, after that resurrection day, nothing in their lives was ever the same again. They were changed forever. Did Jesus change their life circumstances? Not really. Things actually got harder for them from this point forward. But what did change was their view of their circumstances. Their routine would never be the same. Each day would now be greeted through the lens of resurrection. Every mundane moment was now gloriously expectant. As a result, they set the world ablaze with the Gospel message!

A resurrected Jesus is waiting to meet you in the mundane of your routine. A resurrected Jesus is waiting to meet you in your daily drive to work. A resurrected Jesus is waiting to meet you in the battle with your declining health and old age. A resurrected Jesus is waiting to assist you in the fight for your marriage and family.

> I come that they may have life, and have it to the full.
>
> JOHN 10:10

A resurrected Jesus is able to help you break the chains of your addiction. A resurrected Jesus is swimming with you through your sea of doubt. A resurrected Jesus is sitting with you at the desk of the job you hate. A resurrected Jesus is intersecting His strength with your weakness at just the right moment. A resurrected Jesus is walking with you through the "same-old, same-old" of each routine, daily task. That same, resurrected Jesus is able to help you see that even in the hard parts, your life is quite amazing!

The Apostle Paul discovered that same daily resurrection expectation. This is why he stated in Philippians 1:21 (NLT), "For to me, living means living for Christ, and dying is even better."

The stone has been rolled away. The fact that you saw the sun come up today is not due to the routine. It is due to the faithfulness of your God. It means He is not done with you yet. It means He still has something planned for you. He is alive in you! It means your life has a beginning and an end, and everything in between those moments is anything but random or without purpose. Your routine has a design and it is gloriously filled with resurrection moments! Jesus is calling.

It has been said that by their mid-thirties, most people have stopped acquiring new skills and attitudes in any aspect of their lives. How long has it been since *you* acquired a new skill or tried anything new? How many brand-new attitudes have you adopted—personal, political, social, spiritual, or financial? Perhaps you need to adopt some new worship patterns, like lifting your hands, clapping, singing, shouting, or even dancing! Perhaps it's time you try to step out of your comfort zone and serve in a ministry, go on a mission trip, or tell that lost neighbor or co-worker

> For to me, living means living for Christ, and dying is even better.
>
> PHILIPPIANS 1:21

about Jesus. Perhaps it's time to learn a new skill or trade, or you could develop an old talent. Perhaps it's simply time to dare to try something, anything new. You are not too young, too old, or too worn out to try. You are still breathing. You are still here. Your life still has purpose and meaning. As the old saying goes, "Better to try something and fail while daring greatly, than to do nothing and succeed." Be bold and go for it!

Left to routine, you'll easily and imperceptibly fall prey to the "thief's" chief aim: to rob you of your best and most productive years. You'll settle for the dark, mundane cellar, hiding in the basement of security and predictability. Why not come out into the light of abundant living? Pursue the way of Jesus. Accept His approach and live your life with abandon! Don't be afraid to take a few risks! Turn your back on those attitudes and stubborn patterns that prevent you from living a full life. Come alive again! I hope the pages of this book help you find that abundant life.

2
Today

The alarm clock awakens you, sending deafening ripples through your blissful bedtime slumber. You roll over to quiet its intrusive sounds, designed to ensure you start your day on time. For a moment, you'll regret that you ever set the alarm to go off so early. You'll contemplate rolling back over and abandoning the action that prompted you to set the alarm clock. But once you clear the remaining cobwebs of hibernation from your brain, you can make one of the greatest realizations of your day.

Stop and marvel at the profound magnificence that lies before you. Breathe in deeply, look around, listen, and consider that you've been given one of life's greatest gifts: another day. You are breathing; your heart is beating; you are alive! You have been given another chance, another opportunity at life! The journey of TODAY lies before you. Yesterday is behind you. Today, another adventure begins!

> The fact that you woke up is not simply due to the faithfulness of your alarm clock. It is due to the faithfulness of your God.

It doesn't matter what baggage you carried into TODAY from yesterday. TODAY, there will be limitless opportunities before you. Some will be difficult; some will be easy. Some will bring pain, and some will bring joy, but in all of them, you are here, in the battle, in the game, in the fight, for another day. So, get up and swing!

The fact that you woke up is not simply due to the faithfulness of your alarm clock. It is due to the faithfulness of your God. It means He is not done with you. It means He still has something planned for you. It means your life has a beginning and an end, and everything in between those moments is anything but random or without purpose. Even the little things have purpose.

As mundane as you may view your life, it is anything but. You won't be able to define or control every moment, but be assured that every moment defines you. It brings you toward something and makes you ready for something greater and better. For those who trust the Lord and walk in relationship with Him, all of this is pointing us to glory. Everything here is preparing us for there. Everything here is temporary, but it matters. That is the promise of II Corinthians 4:17 (NLT): "For our present troubles are small and won't last very long. Yet they produce for us a glory that vastly outweighs them all and will last forever!"

> For our present troubles are small and won't last very long. Yet they produce for us a glory that vastly outweighs them all and will last forever!
>
> 2 CORINTHIANS 4:17

This moment before you, with a new day ahead of you, is the signal that you are here for a reason. It doesn't matter how old you are. It doesn't matter how sick you are or how debilitated you may be. It doesn't matter what your limitations are. You may be in a time of your life when you regret even waking up. Perhaps guilt or shame overwhelm you. Perhaps worry and anxiety hold you captive. Perhaps you're chronically ill. Perhaps you see the course of events in your life as another opportunity for you to personally screw it up. Perhaps this moment reminds you of how difficult and miserable life can be at times.

But TODAY provides a brand new opportunity to over-come all of that! TODAY is a chance to leave the drudgery behind and strain forward toward what is ahead. TODAY is a gift, whether you see it that way or not. TODAY was never guaranteed to you. Many around you didn't wake up with this gift. One day, your TODAYs will run out; if you know the Lord, it will be time to go home. But if that day is not TODAY, God is still in construction. So, get up and work with it! It's all pointing to something good! Even if you don't feel or see it, you must trust it. That is the work of faith. It's being confident that everything you hoped for will hap-pen. It's being sure of the things you can't see right now. It will come into the fullness of view. Trust that! So, get up and go!

> TODAY is a chance to leave the drudgery behind and strain forward toward what is ahead.

But remember this: TODAY will move forward with or without you. Time waits for no one. The choice is yours. You can grab it by the horns and take all it offers you, or you can roll back over and let it pass you by. The choice is yours. No one else can make that choice for you.

Take the gift and receive all that TODAY has for you, even the parts you don't like. Your face may get muddied, your heart may break at times, but at least you will be in the arena of life. That is the gift. It will offer you moments of bliss and happiness that make you fall in love with it all over again. But it will also force moments upon you that make you question your existence and purpose. But again, that is the arena that lies before you. So, get up, pick up your sword and shield, and walk with purpose!

If you grab TODAY and receive it, your heart will be lifted above the ordinary many more times than it is broken, and those joyful times will sustain you through the broken ones. But the broken ones are not life's way of balancing it all out. They have purpose for you. They will sustain you because they are also redefining you. TODAY, you will learn how to endure anything by redefining everything through the lens God has placed in you. But you have to get up and see it through that lens. The choice is yours.

Before your feet hit the floor, thank the Lord for waking you up and giving you the gift of another day. Thank Him for TODAY. Then ask Him to help you order every moment of TODAY around His will for your life. Even if you make mistakes, TODAY is the sign that God loves you and has not given up on you. Confess and re-pent of your wrongs and mistakes, accept His wonderful offer of grace and mercy, and start over TODAY.

You are loved, you matter, all of this has purpose. It's why you woke up TODAY.

Yesterday has passed, tomorrow is not guaranteed. Right now, you have TODAY. It is not mundane. It is not random. You were made for this. Make the most of every opportunity and don't waste a second!

Breathe in, smile, be confident, be joyful. You are loved, you matter, all of this has purpose. It's why you woke up TODAY. Your joyful blessings will sustain you and remind you of just how beautiful life can be in its fullness. Your sufferings and difficulties will redefine you and strengthen your survival mechanisms. Your weakness will find perfec-tion at the intersection of His strength. Even though you can't explain it, an unexplainable peace will wash over you.

Spend TODAY walking with God and pursuing Him. Do all that you can to put Christ at the center of everything in your life TODAY. This is where your life will find its ultimate joy, peace, and purpose.

God alone has determined the number of TODAY's you will have in this life. Trust the counting of those days and years to Him. In all of the TODAY's that comprise your lifespan, the Lord will handle the length. As He does that, you focus on the depth...and that begins TODAY.

> *"Seventy years are given to us! Some even live to eighty...Teach us to realize the brevity of life, so that we may grow in wisdom."*

Psalm 90:10, 12 (NLT)

3
Yesterday

YESTERDAY has come and gone. YESTERDAY either holds pleasant memories of good times gone by or painful wounds and memories you are glad to see in the rearview mirror. You cannot change YESTERDAY. You cannot relive or recreate YESTERDAY. It has its own untouchable place in the story of our lives. Whether you feel it or not, YESTERDAY has a grand and divine purpose. Many of our YESTERDAYs will be forgotten. Many of our YESTERDAYs will not be forgotten.

> You cannot change YESTERDAY.

Pictures give great graphic reminders of our YESTER-DAYs. Some photos remind us of a time when life seemed perfect and joyful, even for a moment. Other photos remind us of a time when life was anything but perfect. Both have value. We dare not brush over either.

If YESTERDAY has painful memories and wounds, the rearview mirror will have great value. Some painful memories and wounds may be self-induced due to our own harmful choices. Some painful memories and wounds were inflicted upon us due to no choice of our own. Either way, no matter how great the pain, with each new TODAY, we have the great opportunity to see those painful memories grow smaller and smaller in the rearview mirror, as we drive forward with great hope toward TODAY and TOMORROW.

We must drive forward. We have to leave those painful wounds with YESTERDAY. But before we do, we must extract their lessons into the fullness of what is left of our lives. Certainly, those wounds will have extracted pieces of our joy, peace, and sanity. But only for a moment. We can leave the debilitating parts of those extractions with YESTERDAY. We also have the choice to allow the character and hope-building parts of those extractions to make us better. But the choice is ours to make. As difficult as it may be, we must learn before we leave. Once we learn, we have the right and the power to drive away and leave the rest with YESTERDAY—for good.

Those painful memories may even leave scars for a lifetime, but those scars have tremendous potential for indescribable, redemptive beauty with each new TODAY and TOMORROW. Whether that pain produces debilitating wounds that keep us from moving forward from the painful memories of YESTERDAY or become the beautiful scars that tell our redemptive story will be up to us. Your YESTERDAY may be painful, but it can also be the very thing that defines you and gives you great hope for TODAY and TOMORROW.

> Your YESTERDAY may be painful, but it can also be the very thing that defines you and gives you great hope for TODAY and TOMORROW.

Never forget: God's specialty is working painful YESTERDAYs into beautiful TODAYs and TOMORROWs. It is why He sent His Son to this broken world to die for us and be raised again to life. The story of YESTERDAY's cross and empty tomb still produces redemptive stories of untold beauty today and into eternity. No matter what you may be going through, remember that God can make your painful TODAY into a beautiful YESTERDAY.

If your YESTERDAY has pleasant memories, count yourself blessed and take a moment to be thankful. YESTERDAY's joy is a great reminder of God's faithfulness and a platform for a life of gratitude. YESTERDAY's peace can be a source of great fuel, particularly when the circumstances around your TODAY are difficult. YESTERDAY's peace can serve as a great reminder that you've been given the gift of something you didn't earn or even deserve: a satisfying, full life, surrounded by people who love you and that you got to love. There can be no greater gift.

You can no longer live in YESTERDAY, no matter how good or bad it may have been. You cannot dwell in YESTERDAY. It will only leave you stagnant. But you can thank God for YESTERDAY, even the hard parts of it. You can thank God for being faithful and bringing you through each and every YESTERDAY, even when you didn't think you would have a YESTERDAY to talk about or remember.

You cannot re-write YESTERDAY. You cannot go back to it. You may have regrets about it, but those regrets need not keep you trapped and immobilized in the anguish of the sea of unforgiveness. Your regrets about YESTERDAY are a reminder that next to salvation and redemption, you had God's other greatest gift: free will. Regardless of your theological disposition toward free will, God was either using your choices to write His already-revealed story for you, or He was redeeming your choices and working them to good in order to align you with His will for your life. Either way, nothing about your YESTERDAY will be without purpose or meaning, even the parts you would have preferred to avoid.

Finally, this is what leads to the best part about YESTERDAY. If you are still talking or thinking about YESTERDAY, you have TODAY. If your YESTERDAY has produced another TODAY, then God is not done with you yet. It means your story is not over, and God is still writing that story. Yes, He is writing His story through you, and your story is part of that eternal plan of redemption. You are part of history, both now and for eternity.

It doesn't matter how painful or destructive YESTERDAY was or what it produced. If you are still here talking or thinking about it, it means God plans to use it for something beautifully redemptive, far beyond anything you could imagine. It's not over; it's not done; God is still at work. As random, painful, or purposeless as your YESTERDAYs may seem to you, they are not that way to God. Every single YESTERDAY has purpose. Every YESTERDAY has meaning far beyond what you could ever know.

> If your YESTERDAY has produced another TODAY, then God is not done with you yet.

If you have trusted your life to God in faith, then one day, your YESTERDAYs and TODAYs on earth will cease, colliding to be part of God's redemptive plan in eternity. It will be glorious and perfect, and all of it—*all of it*—will make perfect sense. Until then, trust God with your TODAY and allow Him to file your YESTERDAYs into perfect position for His story through your life. Surrender to that, and you will never doubt YESTERDAY.

If you have entrusted and surrendered your life to Him, YESTERDAY is your reminder that God has worked and is working every single event, moment, and rhythm of your life into part of His story for you—the joyful, the painful, the parts you remember, and the parts you don't remember. You have incredible reason to have hope for TODAY and TOMORROW.

As you drive away from YESTERDAY, look at the things growing smaller in the rearview mirror with time and distance, and thank God for His work in redeeming every single one of them. Thank Him for working them to prepare you for the beauty of what lies before of you. It only gets better.

> *"...Forgetting what is behind, I strain forward toward what is ahead. I press on toward the goal to win the prize for which God has called me heavenward in Christ Jesus."*

> Philippians 3:13-14 (NIV)

4

Tomorrow

TOMORROW is not here yet. TOMORROW may never arrive. TOMORROW is not guaranteed. Even if TOMORROW arrives, it may arrive in a much different form than we anticipated. Every one of us is invariably one second from eternity in every moment and situation. One second is all it takes to change everything. That is why nothing about TOMORROW is certain. All that any of us have for certain is the here and now.

TOMORROW can be one of life's greatest blessings and one of life's greatest curses. TOMORROW can be what keeps us from finishing a task that needs to be done sooner than later. However, TOMORROW can also be the thing that gives us hope of making it through the horror of TODAY or YESTERDAY. TOMORROW can make great promises that things will be better and that we will have another chance. Most certainly, that can happen...but it is not guaranteed. We can hope *for* TOMORROW, but we must be wary of hoping *in* TOMORROW. It may not come.

We must meet TOMORROW with the proper perspective, great wisdom, and precision. It can sustain or deceive us. TOMORROW can make us lazy, or it can make us more ardent about what is most necessary. In my humble experience, I have discovered two approaches to the prospect of TOMORROW.

First, it is all too easy to say, "I thought about today... but TOMORROW, or some other day, I will get to it." We must understand that it is a long way to TOMORROW and even longer to someday. TOMORROW should never be a rationalization for apathy, inertia, or laziness. TOMORROW should never be an excuse for a lack of duty, responsibility, or accountability. TOMORROW should never be an alibi for sinking into the abyss of non-living or not fully living for all that TODAY holds. TODAY, the moment in front of us, is the only moment we hold with certainty. But even that can be snatched away in seconds. Never give TOMORROW the power of complacency, at least to the degree that it threatens to produce the stupor of slothfulness or time-wasting.

> TOMORROW should never be an alibi for sinking into the abyss of non-living or not fully living for all that TODAY holds.

Having said that, there is another way to approach TOMORROW. TOMORROW's uncertainty should never be the reason for exhausting TODAY of the things that bring us life. Of course, tasks will need to be done, but there will always be things that need to be done. Many of those things will include things that do not bring us life or enjoyment.

Completing tasks and getting work done teaches us responsibility and accountability. It is in the completion of tasks that we learn to be faithful and trustworthy people who honor our words. However, life is not meant to be lived only in the cycle of finding value in completing tasks, even if our work is what brings us the most enjoyment.

The old saying, "a man (or woman) in motion stays in motion," can be true. It can also be true that a man (or woman) in motion can work themselves to death prematurely, missing much of what was intended to help them live longer, had they taken the opportunity to slow down and experience it.

The reality is that, try as you may, you will never be able to get everything done TODAY. Because TOMORROW is so uncertain, if you view TODAY as the only chance to get everything done, you will risk falling into the abyss of fruitless busyness.

In Western culture, we wear extreme busyness as a badge of honor, as if it adds value to our significance. But it only serves as the opposite. What it really shows is that we are lacking in wonder and awe. It shows that we are incapable of operating in the beauty of tarrying. In such a state, we treat life like a checklist, moving from moment to moment, task to task, without ever pausing to enjoy the moment before us. We are hurried and frantic, which leaves us lifeless and bound, a prisoner to a task-driven life. We think we have achieved something when, in actuality, the only thing we have achieved is locking ourselves in the unknowing and miserable prison of busyness.

> TOMORROW's uncertainty should never be the reason for exhausting TODAY of the things that bring us life.

The problem with this miserable prison is that it leads us to the end of life, having tried so vigorously to get things done that we never really lived at all. In effect, we may have gotten things done, but we never got the most important thing done: living.

There is a fine line in the gift and curse of idleness that TOMORROW can teach us. Being idle as a result of laziness should never be an option. However, there should always be space for idleness in the sense that it can lead us to wonder. Nothingness should never become a lifestyle, but it can be a great gift of refreshment and replenishment. It is in the space and silence of nothingness that we can learn much.

Sometimes, the most productive atmospheres are the ones that are most silent and still.

I am a runner. I am an exercise and competition junkie. The uncertainty of TOMORROW has been a great motivator for me in many sporting and competitive atmospheres. It has given me fuel and adrenaline to push myself beyond what I would have normally done, to go faster and harder.

However, the uncertainty of TOMORROW has also taught me that I can see much more of my surroundings when I am walking through the countryside rather than running through it. I take in much more when I slow my pace. I may have to walk longer to burn as many calories, but I will also contemplate, see, and experience much more than I would in the constant pounding of running. Both have value. Both have their place. Perhaps the same is true of life. You will see and experience so much more when you learn to slow down on occasion.

As did many of us, I grew up on the old saying, "Never put off 'til tomorrow what you can do today." Perhaps that's true in some cases. Perhaps there are more things I could have and should have done. But I also know that there are many joys and life-enriching experiences that I would have never known had I not put something off until TOMORROW.

The beauty and wonder of the here and now rarely gives you a warning sign that you must pull off the road and soak it in. You must learn to recognize those times and be aware of them. You must learn to exist comfortably in those moments. But you will never learn this art until you actually pull off and pause, again and again.

Sure, maybe by putting a few things off until TO-MORROW, I won't get everything done. But maybe, just maybe, I will get more done in the end because I will live longer. This could be much more beneficial to my health than living in the danger of the frantic, stressful pace of a task-driven life. Even if I don't live longer, perhaps I will at least experience the great benefit of quality of life over quantity of tasks completed.

When my three boys were small children, I shared a conversation with an older lady who was a dear friend of mine. I told her of the labor of constantly picking up after my boys and trying to keep the house clean versus taking the time to play with them and just letting them be little boys. She responded with a simple yet profound statement that I never forgot: "Clean houses are overrated. Enjoy every moment with those boys. One day, they will all move out, and you'll long for the days when you barely had the energy to step over another toy."

> If TODAY becomes TOMORROW, then let it point us to the faithfulness of our God and the awareness that He is not yet done with us.

I took her advice to heart. We have a few more dents and stains on the wall, a much dirtier carpet, and a few more dust molecules than I care to see, but oh, the joy of the wrestling and boxing matches, football and basketball games, Nerf gun wars, and runs through the sprinkler! I traded in the task-driven life for a life of building men, and nothing brought me more freedom and joy, even if I did have to deal with stepping over or walking by a few undone tasks.

I am still practicing that today, and a few of those handprints on the wall will never come down, even when the rest of the walls are painted. They remind me that a few of TOMORROW's tasks can wait and that TODAY's divine moments must be given space when they arrive.

There lies the fine art of discerning the lessons that TOMORROW can bring. Only the wisest among us will develop the artistry and finesse to live their lives in a way that distinguishes between wasting time and using time. If TOMORROW teaches us anything, then let it point us to the urgency of TODAY. If TODAY becomes TOMORROW, then let it point us to the faithfulness of our God and the awareness that He is not yet done with us.

Most of all, the most important lesson of TOMORROW should be this one: while nothing about TOMORROW is guaranteed in *this* life, everything about TOMORROW is certain in the life to come. Life does not end with TODAY; we will have a TOMORROW called eternity. Where we spend that eternal TOMORROW depends on what we do with Jesus TODAY. He offers life's greatest gift to us TODAY: salvation, the forgiveness of our sins, a second chance, an abundant and eternal life. That is a TOMORROW that never ends and offers us a hope like no other. If TOMORROW teaches us anything, let it teach us to secure that eternity before TOMORROW becomes TODAY.

> *"For God so loved the world that he gave his one and only Son, that whoever believes in him shall not perish, but have eternal life."*

John 3:16 (NIV)

5

In-Between

Imagine you are standing right on the edge of everything you have ever dreamed and hoped for. It is just within your grasp. You can see it. You can smell it. You can almost touch it. But you have been stopped just short of acquisition. You've been here before. Perhaps you've been here more times than you care to admit. It's the land of the almost, but not just yet. You are neither here nor there. You are in transition. You are…in-between. Sometimes, it seems as if you live here, smack-dab in the middle of the valley of "in-between." You've almost grown used to it. Frankly, you may have grown stale to it. There lies the problem. You've lost the beauty, the mystery, and the wonder of this valley of life called "in-between."

In the Bible there is the story of the Israelites and their exodus from slavery and bondage in Egypt all the way to the land God promised to give them in Canaan. It is an incredible story of God's faithfulness, love, and willful persistence for His people. There are many facets to this story from which we may learn. One in particular is when they came to their own valley of "in-between." The Scriptures record it this way in Deuteronomy 1:19-21 (NLT):

"Then, just as the LORD our God commanded us, we left Mount Sinai and traveled through the great and terrifying wilderness, as you yourselves remember, and headed toward the hill country of the Amorites. When we arrived at Kadesh-barnea, I said to you, 'You have now reached the hill country of the Amorites that the LORD our God is giving us...Go and occupy it as the LORD, the God of your ancestors, has promised you. Don't be afraid! Don't be discouraged!'"

Before entering their promised land, the Israelites sent out a team of spies to scout the land. The scouting mission was not to determine whether to enter the land but to determine the best place in which to enter. It was also to remind the people that the land was a good land, just as God had promised. It was to remind them to continue forward because God is faithful.

Perhaps it would be good to take your own scouting report through the land of God's faithfulness in your own life.

The team of scouts went out, and the rest of the Israelites waited for 40 days and nights. The perseverance of the "terrifying wilderness" was just behind them. They still had the dust from the journey on their sandals, on their backs, and stretched across their faces. They were weary and worn from the journey. Just before them, within reach, was the land God promised, a land "flowing with milk and honey" (Exodus 3:8). But they were stopped short of acquisition. They were neither here nor there. They were in transition. They were in-between.

The scouting team of 12 returned. The land was everything God promised! But ten of them decided that wasn't enough. The land was filled with obstacles and hurdles. It was going to require work and sacrifice. Ten of them spread a negative report that discouraged the people from moving forward. Two of them, having seen the same things, chose an entirely different perspective, saying, "We can do it! The Lord our God is going ahead of us!"

As human nature is prone to do, the people chose to focus on the negative report. They chose to focus on what was wrong rather than what was right. It sent them into a demented frenzy. They refused God's faithfulness, and they refused to enter the land out of fear and hesitation. As a result, that generation (with the exception of the two who believed) never left that valley of "in-between" and died there. It was a sad ending to something that began with such promise.

> Shifting our focus to what's right, rather than what's wrong, will need to be a willful response.

God had protected His people in the plagues of Egypt. He had released them from slavery. He had brought water from a rock for them. He dropped bread from heaven for them to eat each day. He led them with a cloud by day and a fire by night. He never stopped leading them. Just when it looked as if it was all over, standing at the shore of the Red Sea with the world's most powerful army bearing down on them, God did the impossible: He parted the waters and marched them through on dry ground, only to bring the waters back over their enemies to pummel them in defeat. *What else did the Lord need to do?*

But in their fear, they focused more on what was wrong than what had been right all along. In focusing on the negative, they lost sight of God's faithfulness. Sometimes, a loss of memory of God's goodness is the greatest sin we commit. Had they only remembered His faithfulness, how different their lives could have been.

Are you in a valley of "in-between" right now? Are you left always feeling like you are neither here nor there? Do you always feel like you're coming up just short of acquisition? Do you constantly feel like you're stuck in transition? If you are there, I assure you it's not random or without purpose. Perhaps you need to jog your memory. Perhaps it would be good to take your own scouting report through the land of God's faithfulness in your own life.

If you live long enough, you will be jolted with the reality that life is going to provide you with multiple opportunities to focus on what is wrong and bad. That is because this broken world in which we live is littered with deficiencies that, at best, leave us fractured in some way. Some of these moments will be our own doing. We will be responsible for them due to our own poor choices, particularly when we act to please our fleshly desires. But many of them we won't be able to control. They come simply as a result of living in this ruptured world, cluttered with shortcomings.

> I remember my affliction and my wandering, the bitterness and the gall. I well remember them, and my soul is downcast within me.
>
> LAMENTATIONS 3:19-20

The action of looking to, remembering, and celebrating God's faithfulness will come quite easy at times. Birthdays, vacations, Christmas mornings, worship services, weddings, graduations, and the like, all provide moments of bliss that naturally thrust us into the flurry of offering heartfelt thanks to the Lord for such occasions.

But in between these mountain-top experiences, we will ride the lows of the valley, as they rip into us with the force of a tidal wave, leaving us weary and worn to the core. In these times, remembering God's faithfulness will require effort and great intent. Shifting our focus to what's right, rather than what's wrong, will need to be a willful response. We will have to elevate ourselves beyond emotion. We will have to focus on the truths and promises of God that we know, even when we may not currently feel them as strongly as we did in the blissful moments. It will not come easy. We will need to remember the words of the "weeping prophet" Jeremiah in Lamentations 3:19-20 (NIV), "I remember my affliction and my wandering, the bitterness and the gall. I well remember them, and my soul is downcast within me."

It's important to note here that pointing yourself to God's faithfulness does not always need to be a joyful enterprise. But it does need to be willful and hopeful. There will be times in the "in-between" where it may feel as though it requires every ounce of your energy to look to the Source of your hope. It is okay to do it in your mourning. It is okay to be thankful with tears of lament. Sometimes, those tears are the only ones that will provide the healing we need. But look again at the posture of the prophet in Lamentations 3:21-23 (NIV): "Yet this I call to mind and therefore I have hope: Because of the LORD's great love we are not consumed, for his compassions never fail. They are new every morning; great is your faithfulness."

> Yet this I call to mind and therefore I have hope: Because of the LORD's great love we are not consumed, for his compassions never fail. They are new every morning; great is your faithfulness.
>
> LAMENTATIONS 3:21-23

"Yet this I call to mind and therefore I have hope." That phrase does not come naturally. There will be times in the "in-between" where you will have to "call to mind" the Lord's faithfulness. Calling it to mind means taking your own scouting trip. It means choosing to remember and focus on something that may not seem or feel natural. Call it to mind. Purpose to focus on it. Dwell on it. Don't forget it! Go to it in times of distress! It will be the source of your hope.

THE MIRACLE OF THE MUNDANE

When you call this hope to mind, you'll commit it to memory. Then, it will become a habit. It will become your natural response. That natural response will save and guard you in life's most harrowing moments. In the midst of your darkest moments, you'll find the light that points you to God's faithfulness. You'll find that no matter how deep and dark the night, the morning will always rush over you with the reminder that the Lord's compassions and mercies are there for you every morning you awake. They are "new every morning." Hallelujah!

Sometimes, the point of the "in-between" is to remember the "what has been" and the "what is currently." Sometimes, in life, we get so anxious to get to the next thing that we fail to remember the goodness of what has been or even what is happening all around us in the "in-between." Maybe that's why God reminds us in Psalm 46:10a (NIV), "Be still and know that I am God." Some of the best and most epic moments of my life have been in the "in-between" moments.

> Sometimes, the point of the "in-between" is to remember the "what has been" and the "what is currently."

It could be that the reason we never move forward to the next thing is because we refuse to recognize God's faithfulness in the "what has been" and the "here and now." Slow down and be fully aware of your surroundings, even the difficult ones. Be where you are, thank God for His faithfulness, and trust His timing for what is next.

Remember that He is still leading and guiding our steps each day. Remember that He still gives us our daily bread, just what we need and at the right time. He's never late and always on time, even in our impatience. Remember that even when we stand at the water's edge of impossibility, He is able to part the seas of "this can't be done," bring us through on dry ground, and vanquish our enemies behind us. He is still faithful, and He is always able!

Remember that if you are a follower of Jesus, this world in which we live is "in-between." We are in transition. This is not our home. There is an ultimate promised land to come for the believer. As 2 Corinthians 4:17-18 (NLT) says, "These light and momentary troubles are achieving for us an eternal glory that far outweighs them all. So we fix our eyes not on what is seen, but what is unseen." The "in-between" moments are littered with God's faithfulness. Keep your eyes on them, and the glory will come soon enough.

> These light and momentary troubles are achieving for us an eternal glory that far outweighs them all. So we fix our eyes not on what is seen, but what is unseen.
>
> 2 CORINTHIANS 4:17-18

On the Saturday between Jesus' death and resurrection, Jesus' disciples found themselves right in the middle of the valley of "in-between." Everything in their world had been shattered. Their Savior had been crucified on the cross. He had told them He would rise again; three days later. But they were unsure. They could focus on everything that had just gone wrong, or they could focus on everything that was about to go right. They are "in-between." They are waiting. They could focus on God's faithfulness to do what He said He would do, or they could allow their grief to paralyze and overwhelm them.

There were several women (Mary Magdalene, Mary, the mother of James, Joanna, Salome) who knew that even in the midst of their grief and fear, they had to keep moving and functioning. They could only control what they could control. They did what they could and left the rest to God. Luke 23:55-56 (NIV) tells us, "The women who had come with Jesus from Galilee followed Joseph and saw the tomb and how his body was laid in it. Then they went home and prepared spices and perfumes."

These women who followed Joseph of Arimathea to the tomb could not argue for Jesus. They could not rescue Him. They could not overthrow Rome. They couldn't bring Him back to life. They could have been paralyzed by anxiety and stress. But they weren't. Instead, they prepared spices and perfumes with which to anoint the body of Jesus...right there in the valley of "in-between." They couldn't control all of their life circumstances, but did what they could. They focused on doing what they could do, rather than worrying about what they could not do. They remained devoted and left the rest to Jesus. Due to their devotion, they were the first to know about the resurrection when it happened.

The valley of "in-between" still has much to teach us about God's faithfulness. It is not random or without purpose. Keep moving, keep hoping, stay devoted, and focus on what's right rather than what's wrong. Control the things you can control, and leave the rest to Jesus. Like these women, who witnessed the resurrection of Jesus, or like Joshua and Caleb, who led a new generation of Israelites into their promised land, you can bet you'll be pleasantly surprised and overjoyed with what's around the corner. Sunday is always coming! God will always keep His promises! Stay hopeful, remain devoted, and leave it to God, while you wait!

6

Bigger Than You Imagine

You sit imprisoned in your own house. This is what it's come to in your lifespan. The government and ruling authorities have told you where you can and cannot go and what you can and cannot do. The official title is "house arrest." You are trapped in your own rented house. You cannot leave. You are under 24-hour surveillance, and the ruling authorities have appointed guards to stand watch over you inside your own house. They are armed and trained, soldiers who execute justice swiftly if needed. You have no privacy. It is debilitating, but it is far better than the dark, damp dungeon where you have also been imprisoned, chained to walls and other prisoners as your flesh rots and wastes away.

But now, you are here in this confined condition because you would not conform to the narrative of the day. They wanted to conform your language. You refused their demands and spoke anyway. As a result, they eliminated your platforms for speaking. But you could not help but speak what you had been given to speak, that which saved your soul and burns you ablaze with passion. Now, they have restricted your movement and speech.

Having done all this to silence your threat to them, it seems they have made one miscalculation. They underestimated your passion and conviction for that which you speak of so stridently. In eliminating your audience of the populous, they have given you an unsuspecting audience... their own guard. So you speak to the guard. Being assigned to you means they must listen to your ongoing vernacular. Before long your verbal testament has worked its way through the entire guard, and they have all been exposed to your creed. There are even quite a few who have given themselves to this truth you speak of. It's so unlike any other narrative of the day that it has to be believable and worthy of dedication. It's the ultimate turning of the tables. You never imagined it or planned for it. It fell into your lap as a result of your suffering.

They begin to allow you to have visitors. Thankfully, they also allow you to write letters and send them out. That is what you will do. You will write. Your letters will be to converts, many of whom owe their conversion to your efforts to convey the message. You will write to gatherings of people who have been transformed like you and given their lives over to this timeless confession. These letters, written from prison, become part of your everyday experience. They are written to correct, encourage, and build up those who are laboring in the great effort. You write one letter to a Roman colony called Philippi.

Unknown to you, you will be in this location under house arrest for approximately two years. It is much longer than you would have ever imagined. When the appropriate times have come to their conclusions, the inevitable you knew would come will arrive. They will march you out to the place of execution, and with the violent crash of a sword or axe, they will behead you. You will become a martyr because you were willing to die for the thing they tried to steal from you.

In what they thought they were taking, you were actually given more. When they thought they had taken the grand audience from you, you were given a strategic audience appointed to you: their own soldiers. Through their supposed limitations on you, they increased your reach far beyond anything you would have thought possible.

They thought they had reduced you to a broken-spirited jailbird, whose letters only reached a handful of meaningless house churches in Philippi. But since that time, billions of people have read and memorized the 2,183 words of that letter to those churches. They have quoted them at weddings, funerals, and used them for sustenance in their own times of peril. The words of that letter have been put into more than five billion Bibles and printed in more than 1,551 languages all over the world. Not to mention all of the other letters you wrote from varying locations to varying peoples, in which the same exact thing happened.

> He is always working, always winning. He is the King! He is Jesus!

The reason this happened is because the God you serve has plans and is fulfilling those plans until He returns to earth to rule and reign with His Church and establish His New Kingdom. None of those plans will ever be thwarted, no matter the efforts set against them. You will be remembered as the Apostle Paul, the guy who tried ferociously to abolish the Church of Jesus Christ but became so convinced of the Gospel of Christ that you ended up defending His Church. You ended up planting more of the Churches you initially tried to destroy. Ultimately, you gave your life for the cause you once tried to destroy. It was all bigger than you ever imagined.

Stay faithful saints. He is the God who takes the little and menial things we do in love and faith on a daily basis, and turns them into something bigger than we could imagine. He is always working, always winning. He is the King! He is Jesus!

> *"I want you to know, brothers, that what has happened to me has really served to advance the gospel, so that it has become known throughout the whole imperial guard and to all the rest that my imprisonment is for Christ. And most of the brothers, having become confident in the Lord by my imprisonment, are much more bold to speak the word without fear."*

Philippians 1:12-14 (ESV)

7

The Best Haircut I Ever Had

One of my favorite things to do as a child was get a five-dollar bill from one of my parents, get on my bicycle, and ride the three blocks from my house up to Broome's Barber Shop for a haircut in downtown Waxhaw, NC, where I grew up. There was nothing like the warmth of the shaving cream lathered across the back of my neck and the whisk of the razor blade as it glided through the cream, slowly turning up and over my ears. A heavy wipe of a damp, cool towel soon gave way to the coolness of the breeze across my freshly trimmed ears and neck as I stepped down off the wooden board that stooped me up high enough so that the town barber, Wade Broome, could effectively trim every hair. Talking about fire engines with the old barber and hearing the conversations of the old men who visited the picturesque old barber shop was icing on the cake. I always learned something new with each trip.

But this warm, early afternoon summer trip as a nine-year-old would be one I would never forget. Every now and then, if it was open, I would enter through the back door of the barber shop, just to change things up and let people know I was a regular. I decided to do so on this day. Much to my surprise, the barber shop stood completely empty and deafly quiet, with the front door standing wide open. This was an unlikely circumstance, particularly given the time of day. Normally, the barber shop would be bustling with business, along with a group of old men sitting around shooting the breeze. It was strangely void of any activity, with the front screen door standing wide open. The only sign of life was the box fan circulating air through the room.

Curious, I eased toward the front screen door to see why it stood open. Just on the other side of the door, I could hear voices slowly beginning to rise with emergence. I figured I needed to let Wade the barber know I was his latest customer. I walked through the front door and right out onto the sidewalk running through the middle of town. It was at that instance my heart dropped into the pit of my stomach, and I realized what I had walked into at that moment.

To my left, I saw Wade standing with his hands raised in front of his face. His voice was urgent yet strangely compassionate and calm. "Freddie, just put down the gun. Everything's gonna be alright. Let's work this out together."

As I peered directly to my right, there was a large man walking toward the barber with a shotgun in his hands, pointed, loaded, and ready to fire. I realized I was the only thing between the gunman and the barber.

We were surrounded by a bunch of other older men on the street and sidewalk who were all saying the same thing, "Freddie, just put down the gun. It's gonna be alright. We'll be alright together."

Is this really happening!? I said to myself. Yes, it was happening. I had somehow stumbled right into the middle of it. Freddie was from a poor family. He had no money. He wanted food from the corner grocery store down the street, so he decided to rob the store. As he came out onto the street, this group of men from the barber shop met him. I can't recall for sure, but I'm fairly certain the Waxhaw Police Force consisted of just two police officers at that time.

They shared one car, and only one was on duty at a time. You had to dial seven digits to get the police or emergency crews. There would be no help coming right away. This was the situation.

The barber looked at me gently and said, "Mark, just go on back in the barbershop, and we'll get you fixed up quick."

The gunman continued to come. I froze. The men continued to talk to Freddie and press into the situation. That gun could have blown a hole through any of us. I waited for the worst. All of a sudden, Freddie dropped to his knees and handed the gun over to Wade. The other men stepped in and put their arms on his shoulders to secure the situation. "It's gonna be alright, Freddie. I understand," said the brave barber, "but you just can't rob a store."

Just as Freddie nodded his head and his tears began to flow, the police car finally arrived. The lone police officer handcuffed Freddie, told him it would be alright, and placed him into the back seat of the car. They drove away. Everyone walked back into the barbershop. Wade pulled out the board, looked at me, and said, "Now, hop on up here!"

Wanting the gruesome details, I asked him, "What happened?"

His only reply was, "Freddie was just having a bad day. People can do some pretty rough things when they get desperate." That was all that was said. The scissors and clippers began to whap, the shaving cream lathered up, and the old men went back to talking.

Freddie, Wade, and all the old men had grown up together, gone to school, played on the playgrounds, and worked in the farm fields and the factories. They all went to church in that town, went off to fight the same wars, and came back to try and scratch a living in that small town with the water tower at its center.

Strangely, no one else at the scene pulled any guns that day. No shots were fired. Tempers didn't even seem to flare.

The situation was dire and could have gone another way. The streets could have been filled with blood that day. No one ever said anything about the fact that Freddie was a black man and the barber was a white man. There were no cell phones recording the incident. There were no social media posts. There was no media coverage. There were no politicians sweeping in to give comment. Just small-town people doing what they do and helping each other when one of their own was having one of the worst days of his life. I didn't even tell my parents what happened until many years later.

As I got on my bicycle to ride home that afternoon, I thanked the Lord I was still alive. I realized that anyone can have a really bad day or moment. I learned that everyone needs a measure of grace and forgiveness. We're all just a few decisions or circumstances from a desperate situation, and few of us know how we'll react until we get there. I realized we all need God, and He's big enough for all our brokenness. I realized that the foot of Jesus' cross is the only place any measure of rebuilding and reconciliation begins. I realized that life is littered with heroes who seek to do the right thing in the everyday moments of life and never seek any recognition.

For a while, I wondered if that moment I had experienced was some distant utopia or foreign hope that is far from reality. I wondered if I had imagined it. Maybe it was some movie scene I dreamed about in a scene from Mayberry. It was only a few short years later that I rode my bike by the old barbershop one summer afternoon in downtown Waxhaw. There stood old Wade the barber, laughing and talking with Freddie. As the warm breeze swept across my face, I smiled and kept peddling. It really happened that way. It was a routine day with ordinary people sharing life experiences, all helping each other along the way. These are some of life's most exciting and miraculous moments.

Life Lessons

8

Own Your Stuff

The flames raged and pounded against the side of the house. They rose to the rooftop of the one-story, three-bedroom, ranch-style house that our neighbors called home in Waxhaw, NC. They grew up next to us, the only other house on Bivens Street. The natural areas and bushes lining the backside of their home were already burnt to a crisp. The flames now threatened to consume the rest of the house. I suspect they would have already begun devouring the house had it not been made of brick. The moment my sister and I saw the flames, we cried out and sprinted back to our house, which sat just 50 yards from the home threatening to burn to the ground. I outran my sister to the front door and alerted my parents to the emergency that had suddenly been thrust into our laps. The moments that followed were some of the most frightening of my life.

Let's back up about an hour from this moment. It was the 4th of July. As was our tradition, my aunt and uncle, along with my cousins, all gathered with us to wrap up our patriotic celebration with the grand finale of shooting off fireworks from the street in front of our house. I might add that fireworks were as illegal in North Carolina back then as they are today. I might also add that people broke that law as frequently back then as they do today. At the time, we were one of the lawbreakers.

The night ended well, the fireworks were great, and another year seemed in the books as far as the 4th of July goes. My cousins, along with my aunt and uncle, all left to go home. My parents began to clean up. My sister and I went to walk the dog around the block. That's when we saw the flames raging and threatening to burn down our neighbor's house. I often wonder how different my life would be had we not decided to go walk the dog on that unforgettable July 4th evening.

I ran into the house and alarmingly notified my parents that the neighbor's house was on fire! Our neighbors had a house at the lake, which is where they were every 4th of July. They weren't even home. The water hose at their house was on the end where the flames were ablaze. It was of no use; our water hose didn't stretch that far. After calling the fire department, which was a seven-digit call in those days, we knew our only hope was to carry buckets of water from our house to the flames until the fire truck got there.

My sister and I began filling up bucket after bucket of water from the hose attached to our house. My mom and dad ran like Olympic sprinters with buckets of water in hand from our house to the neighbors in an attempt to quench the flames. We were like a well-oiled fire brigade! Actually, we were just desperate and filled with adrenaline. Nonetheless, with a little help from heaven, we were able to extinguish the flames before the fire department arrived. And they were only about a 5-10-minute walk from our house.

The fire department arrived and inspected the house thoroughly. They sprayed down the impacted area to make sure there was nothing smoldering that would reignite. The town was still small enough at the time that we knew every person at the fire department. A friend of the family then walked around the corner with a burned bottle rocket in hand and said, "I think I have the culprit for your fire." In the darkness of that Independence Day, I watched my dad bow his head. The next few moments were deflating and embarrassing for us all. There were few words.

To be fair, there were lots of people from the neighborhood on the other side of our neighbor's house shooting off fireworks as well. That bottle rocket could have come from anywhere. But my dad took responsibility for it. He owned it all. The natural areas and all the bushes would have to be replanted. The black soot from the flames on the side of the house would have to be cleaned and pressure-washed. But thank God, that was the only damage. The house was spared and left standing with no further damage, not even to the roof.

The three days that followed were weary and long as we waited for our neighbors to return home from the lake. Raeford Couick and my dad had bought that stretch of land together and built their houses next to each other. They grew up together in that town. They were the best of friends. And now, my dad's family had almost burnt his friend's house down by carelessly shooting off fireworks on the 4th of July.

I'll never forget the day they returned and my dad walked over to tell them what happened. We didn't know what would happen next. Almost an hour went by before my dad came back. We waited anxiously, wondering what must be happening. He returned. There were no black eyes, bruises, or blood. But minutes later, there were police cars in the driveway of my neighbor, taking a report.

Again, my dad owned all of it. When he walked over to their house, he didn't call up my uncle, who had also been shooting fireworks with us, to go with him. He didn't take any of us with him. He didn't talk about the other neighbors. He took responsibility for it all. He paid for the bushes and natural areas to be replanted and for the house to be cleaned. My allowance was unaffected. He owned it all. He took responsibility for what he had done wrong—for what *we* had all done wrong. Eventually, their friendship was restored, and things went back to normal.

I'll never forget the look on my dad's face over those next several days. Several years later, after battling alcoholism for more years than I can count, I would see that look again when, after getting arrested for a DUI, my dad stood at the end of a long hallway in front of a jail cell and told my mom "I'm so sorry" after she came to bail him out of jail. I saw the same look days later when he was showing me the bed he shared in a room full of other recovering alcoholics and drug addicts at a rehab facility in Union County, NC. Again, he took responsibility, and he owned it all.

> He never made excuses, never blamed anyone else, and never played the role of victim. When you mess up, take responsibility and own it.

There was only so much he could do to repair the damage from that fateful July 4th evening. There was only so much he could do to repair the emotional damage we all suffered from his addiction for so many years. But he took responsibility and did as much as he could do on his end. When he fell down, he owned it and got back up. He never made excuses, never blamed anyone else, and never played the role of victim.

Surprisingly, though none of us would ever wish to walk through those broken-world experiences willingly, when we did, we found a fortitude and grace that left us better than we were before they took place. That grace offered by others and, most importantly, by the Christ that we followed is what sustained us and ultimately set us free to resume life with joy. Life was much sweeter because of it.

My 4th of July lesson had little to do with patriotism, walking dogs, shooting off fireworks, or even breaking the law. It was simply this: when you mess up, take responsibility and own it. Do what you can to mend it. But realize you'll only be able to do so much, and that is natural. Some of the hurt from those consequences of broken-world choices serves to remind us that for followers of Jesus, this broken world is ultimately not our home. This truth leads to the best part: if you're truly repentant, while you may or may not get the grace you so desire from the offended or the people you hurt, you'll always get it from your Savior, Jesus. Accept that truth, and you'll discover how amazing His grace can be, particularly when you find that you're the "wretch" the old hymn ("Amazing Grace") is talking about.

9
Bloodletting

The strand of rubber wrapped tightly around my arm, enlarging a vein perfectly suited for what was needed. The needle made its way into my vein with relative ease and began to extract blood, totaling four small vials. The nurse then completed the process by placing a bandage over the puncture where the extraction occurred. I was done. They would test the blood to see if I was a match.

The process leading up to this moment had been arduous, dominating my life and thoughts for several weeks. It was something only my family knew. My uncle had been battling a cancer that would take his life without a stem-cell transplant. In searching through the millions of people in a donor database, they were unable to find even one match. The next course of action was to turn to his extended family. Without a donor and the hope of a successful transplant, he would die.

As with anything, stem-cell transplants present risks to the donor. Not only is there a physical risk, but there is also the time, physical, and emotional investment it takes. Perhaps that explains why there were few takers when asked. It's not as simple as a prick of the finger. Thankfully for my uncle, while I was a 50% match, they were able to find a 100% match, which his body was most likely to accept.

It's a fascinating medical miracle: the fact that you can take blood and stem cells from one person and inject them into an entirely different person who is sick. If the sick person's body accepts the blood and the cells contained in it, their body will begin to build an entirely new blood and immune system, which will make them well again. They will essentially be a brand new person because of someone else's blood. The other person's blood and code will be on the inside of them, surging with new life. Their sickness will be made well, and they will be brand new, totally transformed. Amazing!

I will not deny that laboring and praying over the thought of the transplant process prior to giving blood was heavy for me. I was not terribly close to this uncle. I wouldn't hesitate if it were my mom, dad, wife, or kids, but an uncle I rarely see? The thought that motivated me most was, *What if I were in his shoes, and he was one of a few potential people who were my only hope?* I would hope he would do the same for me.

For those who place their faith in Him, Jesus offers a new beginning and a new life. We have a Savior who died o bring us near to God and into a relationship with Him *out of love.*

Of course, this brings me to the prayer of Jesus in the garden of Gethsemane, recorded in Matthew 26. Jesus prayed this prayer, moments before He would go to shed His own blood for our sin, in our place, so that we might have life. He said, "Abba, Father, for you all things are possible; remove this cup from me; yet, not what I will, but what you will" (Matthew 26:39-NIV).

As much weight as I was feeling with my own process of giving blood, I can only imagine Jesus' weight at that moment in the garden. The physician himself, Luke, records that the weight was so unimaginable and Jesus prayed with such heaviness that His "sweat was like drops of blood falling to the ground" (Luke 22:44). This condition is known as hematidrosis. It is a rare condition in which the capillary blood vessels that feed the sweat glands rupture, causing them to exude blood. It only happens under extreme physical and emotional stress.

We know how the story ends. Jesus would go to the cross, shed His blood, and give His life for our rescue from sin and death. He would be victoriously raised to life only three days later, and He now sits at the right hand of God the Father.

There are *zero* reasons to feel you are unloved, abandoned, unwanted, or that your life has no purpose.

For those who place their faith in Him, Jesus offers a new beginning and a new life, freeing us from the curse of sin and death forever. Similar to a stem-cell transplant, when we give our lives to Jesus, His resurrection life comes in, soars through our veins, and creates an entirely new person. His life-giving blood makes us new in spirit. The old, sin-sick life is gone, and a new and redeemed life has begun. It's as if we are a brand-new person with a brand-new strand and code from heaven now living on the inside of us. That is an amazing thought!

What's even more amazing is to consider Romans 5:8, which states that Christ died for us "while we were still sinners." In other words, He died for us at our worst moment, while we were at our worst, on our worst day. I can tell you honestly that if the person on the other end of my own minor blood-letting venture was a terrorist or someone who had lived a horrible life, I would not have been sitting in that hospital room giving blood for them, nor would I have made the trip.

Yet, we have a Savior who died the bloodiest, most horrible death ever known to man in our place when we were at our worst moment, furthest from God. He died to bring us near to God and into a relationship with Him *out of love.* Even more amazing is that in Hebrews 12:2, the Bible says that Jesus did it "for the joy set before Him." *Joy?* Yes, joy. There are no appropriate words for this sacrifice.

The only logical response is to receive it, accept it, and give your life to it out of the same loving motivation that was given for you. There are *zero* reasons to feel you are unloved, abandoned, unwanted, or that your life has no purpose.

Jesus is real. His cross and resurrection are real. You will never convince me otherwise. His life-transforming blood is the only answer for our broken world. It was the only hope for **The blood makes** my broken life. In many ways we are **everything new!** sick with a sort of spiritual cancer. Without life-saving blood, we will die a spiritual death. He offered His blood on our behalf. When we receive and trust Him as Savior, His blood surges through us. His life becomes our life. We get a new code. We get another chance, a brand-new life. It doesn't matter how sick we were. We become a new person. What an amazing grace!

In response, we spend the rest of our lives in gratitude to Him by loving Him, serving Him, sacrificing as He sacrificed, and giving up as He gave. We try to continuously gather with other people who have the same spiritual blood surging through their veins, and with great passion, together, we worship the God who saved us all.

In response, we tell as many people who will listen that there is a rescue for this dreadful cancer of sin, and we lead them to it. We lead them to the One who first gave His blood for us, and we tell them that He offers eternal life for all who believe. There is no other transplant or procedure that compares. It requires no medical insurance and can be received by faith. The results are guaranteed and life-transforming. The blood makes everything new!

10
Failure

I still remember the day I went to get my driver's license for the first time as a young 16-year-old teen. I use the word "first" because I had to do it twice. The first time, I went into the DMV just like every other excited and expectant teenager. The instructor came out with a clipboard, called my name, and off I went with her for the driving part of the test. I had already aced the written and road sign tests. All that was left was that dreaded three-point row turn.

I navigated that entire driving test perfectly. Right-hand turn signal, then the left, check the rear-view mirror, and keep it between the lines. With great precision, I mastered the challenge of the three-point row turn. Bring me my license, baby; I'm on my way!

As I drove back into the DMV parking lot, the instructor calmly said, "Just pull in and park next to this car." *Easy enough,* I thought. Then, out of nowhere, *"Boom!"* The unthinkable happened. I did the absolute worst thing you can do on a driver's test: I bumped into another car in the parking lot. I had aced every single test until this moment when I bumped into a non-moving vehicle in the parking lot—with the driving instructor from the DMV sitting right beside me! My head sank into my chest.

The instructor calmly but firmly said, "Well, wait two weeks, and then you can come back and retest. Now, go inside and see if you can find the driver of that car." Then she got out and walked back inside. It was as low as I've ever felt. It was even worse telling my dad what happened as he walked out of the lobby, assuming I was about to get my license.

I swore my dad to secrecy. If any of my friends were to find out about this, I'd be ruined. I spent the next two weeks in absolute dejection. But I also began the task of working and preparing myself to go back and try again. Two agonizing weeks passed, and my dad asked if I was ready to go back. I didn't want to go back. I didn't care if I ever drove a car again at that point. But I knew I had to go back, or I would be frozen by fear and failure for the rest of my adult life.

> I knew I had to go back, or I would be frozen by fear and failure for the rest of my adult life.

I'd like to tell you I went with brave confidence, but I didn't. I went with a plan of what I was going to do if I failed again. I went with a prayer that I would not get that same instructor. God answered the second half of the prayer the way I prayed it.

As I walked into the DMV, I was relieved to find no sign of that previous instructor, but God didn't take away my nervous trepidation. Instead, the Lord taught me a different lesson that day. Needless to say, I passed the test and didn't play demolition derby with any other cars in the parking lot. I was relieved.

Passing the test and getting my driver's license was actually not the thing that made me the most joyful that day. I was more jubilant over the fact that I had found enough courage to pick myself up and go back to the DMV for a second chance. For sure, I was relieved and happy to get my driver's license. But what mattered more to me was the fact that I found the courage to go back to the DMV and try again, even though I feared I might fail a second time.

In 2 Corinthians 4:8-12 (NIV), the Apostle Paul wrote, "We are hard pressed...perplexed...persecuted...struck down." But he followed each one of those statements with the response of "but not crushed...but not in despair...but not abandoned...but not destroyed." I know the context here is more about difficulty and suffering than about failure, but it sounds like Paul knew a little bit about getting back up, even when everything around him was telling him to stay down.

> Don't let any failure keep you from getting back up and trying again, and again, and again.

For me, that moment at the DMV is minuscule in comparison to what the Apostle Paul faced in his own life. It's even minuscule compared to the other struggles and failures I've faced in my life since then. But it did teach me how to approach struggles and failures. Yes, part of life is learning to overcome our fears and failures. But part of life is also having the courage to get back up and keep moving forward courageously and confidently, even if you're still scared to death or you keep getting knocked back down.

For me, the greatest teaching moment at the DMV that second time was not walking out with my license in hand. The teaching moment was getting in the car at the beginning of the second driving test and being willing to turn the key in the ignition and try again, even if it meant I might fail another time.

Strangely, it wasn't until the moment that the car turned on and the second test began that all my fear went away. I didn't need to achieve perfection anymore. My success was defined by more than results. I just needed to prove to myself that I was at least willing to show up and get back in the battle.

Success for me that day was needing to know I was willing to get back up, keep fighting, and keep pressing on. Failure taught me a valuable lesson at that stage of my life. You may go down or make mistakes, but get back up and keep moving. Don't let any failure keep you from getting back up and trying again, and again, and again.

Fear is natural. But never let it paralyze you into submission or keep you from moving forward. You'll find that if you're willing to put the key in, turn the ignition, and put it in drive, you will always have the potential to go further than you did the first time.

11

Winning Is Not A Score

I finished a tearful embrace with my son's high school basketball coach. When I saw my firstborn son, Jadon, come out of the locker room a moment later, I broke into more tears. He was a senior in high school. They had lost their playoff basketball game in the state tournament. The realization that this would be his last high school basketball game, and the last time he wore the Mt. Pleasant jersey, hit me harder than I anticipated. The finality of it all didn't make me sad; I was overwhelmed with gratitude for the entirety of the journey and the fact that we got to be part of it. These were not tears of sadness but thankfulness and joy. The scoreboard above us indicated we had lost, but nothing could have been further from the truth.

Winning is not a score. We're taught to believe it is because the team or individual with the most points on the scoreboard wins in virtually every athletic competition other than golf. While it's true that there are winners and losers in every competition, the scoreboard is only one small, inconsequential part of defining a win. The scoreboard said that we were on the losing end. The truth is that we left the building as winners that night. Not just the players but their families as well.

Did we drive two hours up and back to lose that game? No, we drove those hours because we were part of something bigger than ourselves. We were part of a community, a family sharing joy and heartache, wins and setbacks—together. Some experiences left us jumping for joy, while others were heart-wrenching and left us in tears. But we shared them together, and together matters because it makes us accountable and responsible. We stood, fell, and picked each other up together. It was our town, our team, our kids—together. We were better because of *together*. Winning is not a score.

Some of these kids started their journey together in junior high school. They had been playing together for almost 2,200 days. That's a long time. They had built relationships and shared experiences where life is lifted above the ordinary. They had worked together, played together, and spilled sweat, blood, and tears together. They probably thought it would always be the same—but it wouldn't. Some of their friendships would deepen over the years, but many would become a distant memory as they grew apart. But they will always be able to say that they had these moments together.

> We were better because of *together*. Sometimes it's more important to be in relationship than to always be right.

The older they grow, the more they will understand there will never be anything like it again. They may even play sports at the next level, but none will be as pure. Those memories and that realization will drive them to deeper gratitude. If they're smart enough, they will grab hold of that moment, leading them to prioritize thankfulness and humility. Winning is not a score.

One day, they will find themselves at the end of a receiving line at the funeral home or the bottom of some life crisis. But because of what they shared here with this group and these families, they will find the hand of one of their old teammates reaching out to grab, embrace, and help them through dark times. No scoreboard can equate to that. Winning is not a score.

Their school is not a fortress for high school basketball. Talented kids generally transfer to find better opportunities. They had a few leave, endured a coaching change, and often found themselves on the underside of respect. But those who stayed and committed themselves to the process learned the value of covenant and commitment. They learned that love, passion, and surrender are choices, regardless of your environment. This will matter one day when they're considering walking out on a marriage or family situation that isn't meeting their expectations. It will matter when their church didn't do it the way they thought it should be done. It will matter when it's not going the way they wanted in every situation of life. They will find the value of sticking it out, working through it, and making it better; everyone around them will be better for it. They will learn that sometimes it's more important to be in relationship than to always be right. Winning is not a score.

There was a moment in the summer league, before the season even started, when one of their starting seniors went down with a ligament tear in his knee. The realization hit hard that he would not be back and would lose his senior season of basketball. Tears flowed and hearts sank; it was a blow to the entire team. It was a devastating blow to that family. Yet, all year, his teammates watched that kid show up to every game, sitting on the bench to cheer them on, even though he knew he wasn't getting a minute of playing time. His teammates watched his family show up to every game to cheer them on because they'd been there from the beginning, even though they knew their own son would never set foot on the floor. His family even worked the concession stand multiple times. They poured in, gave back, and gave up as if their son was playing. Their posture never changed. Because of this, some of the most memorable moments of the season weren't even on the hardwood. They happened every time that family showed up to sit in the stands or serve in the concession booth. Together, we all learned that you can remove your adversity, or you can redeem it. They chose to redeem theirs, and we were all better for it. Winning is not a score.

Speaking of memorable moments, one is indelibly etched in my memory: the night another of the starting seniors went to the floor, also with a torn ligament. Now, only a third of the way through the schedule, he would also lose his season.

As he lay on the floor agonizing in pain, we hoped and prayed for the best, but we knew it was not good. That's when I watched his dad pick him up and carry him all the way across the floor to the locker room. I could see all the dreams that would be left undone and unrealized on his face. I knew all he had poured into his son's basketball journey. The moment he carried his broken son across that floor will never leave me. That could have just as well been me. But that family also returned the next game, the next, and the next, and the rest of them. That kid sat on the bench and cheered the rest of the team on as well. Adversity redeemed always has more value than adversity removed.

> You can remove your adversity, or you can redeem it.

I realized of all the titles I could achieve in life, none would be more valuable than "Dad." One day, if they're blessed enough, these boys will have kids who fall in life and end up with broken situations and circumstances. They may even disappoint. But they'll have the memory of the night that father carried his broken boy across the floor.

That will remind us all to never give up on our kids or other people, even if it means we have to carry them. Winning is not a score.

Finally, they'll look back one day and realize that they were never supposed to be where they were. No one expected them to finish third in the conference and make the state tournament, particularly with all the adversity they faced. But they did it.

One day, they'll be in another situation with someone telling them they don't deserve to be there, and they'll remember that they've done it before and can do it again. They will always fight, always claw, and never give up. They will realize they are not a failure, no matter what. The fight is always worth it. Their effort matters. Winning is not a score.

> Never give up on your kids or other people, even if it means you have to carry them.

They shared it all—the practices, the bus rides, the pizza, the laughter, the tears, the wins, the losses, the hugs, the high-fives. One day, they'll look back and realize there isn't anything like it, and they'll be thankful they had it. Maybe they'll be standing at the end of a locker room watching their own kid come out for the last time, and they'll shed tears they didn't expect to shed because they're overwhelmed with gratitude. It won't matter as much what the scoreboard says at that moment because winning is not a score. The wins and losses won't matter nearly as much as every lesson they learned in the mundane moments apart from the final score. Because winning isn't always a score; it's so much more.

12

Celebrate Anyway

In the time of the great COVID-19 pandemic of 2020/2021, like so many, after being diagnosed with COVID-19, my wife and I completed our two-week quarantine. Though they didn't get the virus, our boys had to do the same thing. Our symptoms lasted about 18 hours, and that was pretty much it; it was over. After that, it was 13 days of staying locked up, feeling perfectly fine.

However, there was one set of symptoms that stuck around like an unwanted guest: my loss of taste and smell. For someone who enjoys the beauty of eating and savoring good food, this was not the most pleasant of experiences, particularly when so many in our church family took care of us and blessed us with such great meals during our sickness. My boys were in digestive jubilation!

After being confined to the walls of our house, without any access to the outside world for two weeks, we were ready to resume normal flight patterns. One must understand, though feeling perfectly normal, I spent the entire two weeks eating every meal at a card table set up in my bedroom, all alone. When it was all over, we decided to go out and celebrate with a meal together, all at the same table together again. Anywhere other than that card table would do. Anywhere other than the walls of our 14-day confinement would do. This was worthy of a celebration.

We would laugh; we would talk; we would revel in simply doing what we've always taken for granted: the marvel of sitting beside and across from each other at a dinner table. I would not be able to taste or smell a large portion of that celebratory meal. It would not have the normal, desired outcome. As a matter of fact, as far as taste buds go, there would be little outcome. I would just have to imagine the greatness of the meal. One could suggest it would be wise to delay any such celebration until I could fully realize or enjoy it. But that would miss the point.

There is always room to celebrate the journey even before you get the desired outcome. Sadly, this is one of the great things we miss in the mundane moments of life. We wait until the outcome is certain before we celebrate. We miss so much in not celebrating the process.

We won't always get to choose the circumstances that befall us in life, but we will get to choose how we approach those circumstances.

There are also times when we celebrate the outcome long before it's fully realized, or even when the natural circumstances don't warrant a celebration. Several weeks before my own COVID-19 diagnosis, I led funeral services for a long-time friend whose outcome from COVID-19 had a tragic ending. After a brief fight he would not survive. Unexpectedly, the world of the family he left behind was turned upside down. The outcome was not the one we desired.

And yet, there we stood together, singing songs of God's grace and provision, celebrating a life of well-lived faithfulness. There were tears, smiles, songs, and even a few laughs. The days ahead would still be difficult. The outcome of that moment would only be fully realized in eternal glory.

But it was still a moment worthy of celebration for the hope and glory to come, a hope and glory that these temporary afflictions on earth were producing for us. That was still worthy of a celebration, even in the difficulty of undesirable circumstances.

We won't always get to choose the circumstances that befall us in life, but we will get to choose how we approach those circumstances. We get to choose our perspective and posture toward those circumstances and how we celebrate them.

I remember the first meal I ate with my dad after his second cancer diagnosis. I wanted to soak my napkin with tears of sorrow and heartbreak. But strangely, in the unexplainable peace of that moment, we chose to celebrate. We didn't celebrate the diagnosis of cancer, but we did celebrate the fact that God had been with my dad in his first battle with cancer. We celebrated that He was not going to abandon us and that we would not face the second bout of cancer alone. Many times, we must celebrate the process, even before the outcome is realized. You may not want to celebrate, but you have to do it anyway. There is always room for celebration.

> Many times, we must celebrate the process, even before the outcome is realized.

In Luke 14:15-24, Jesus tells a story about a man who throws the celebration of all celebrations. But then, every event planner's greatest fear comes true: the refusals come pouring in, and no one shows up to celebrate. They all give woeful excuses for not celebrating. We tend to do the same with Jesus' offer of salvation.

But the host refuses to be defeated. There *will* be a celebration! So he sends his servant out into the streets to pull in the "poor, the crippled, the blind, and the lame." Then, to get even more people, he goes out into the roads less traveled, inviting the forgotten who live there. He wants the house full. The celebration goes on, even with the rejection from so many. It's interesting that the ones filling up the table of celebration are the ones who have the most reasons not to celebrate.

Jesus litters life with opportunities to celebrate, but few grab hold of them because they're waiting for the desired outcome. The invitation to celebrate came to those who were still in the midst of their brokenness and residing in their affliction. Yet, in accepting God's invitation to celebrate, even in the midst of undesirable circumstances, they found room at the table for their mourning to be turned to dancing, as Psalm 30:11 so eloquently phrases.

> Our worship celebrations are so void of life because our lives are so void of celebration.

Our worship celebrations are so void of life because our lives are so void of celebration. We focus on the limitations of our obstacles rather than the resources of our faithful God. We meander through the mundane, existing from moment to moment, rather than stopping to celebrate the cluster of God's goodness in the mundane. Things don't always have to fall perfectly into place for celebration or worship to happen. Sometimes, the most powerful celebrations and the most powerful worship services take place when everything is breaking apart. We should never wait to celebrate.

Once we learn to celebrate in the mundane before the outcome is certain, our celebrations will become worshipful. When that happens, our worship will become celebratory. When that happens, we won't have enough seats to hold the people who want to get into our sanctuaries of worship.

The practice of celebrating before the desired outcome will change our posture and perspective, moving us forward. So, even when the world declines it, celebrate! When everyone prioritizes it away, celebrate! When the pain, hurt, and gloomy forecast try to suppress your joy, celebrate! There is always room at the table for the broken to celebrate. It is there that the Lord takes away our clothes of mourning and trades them for clothes of joy in spite of our circumstances.

That day we went to dinner after our COVID-19 quarantine, I couldn't taste it, but I celebrated with food anyway. Sure, it wasn't the same, but it was still worthy of a celebration. It was my way of rebelling against the world's system of gloom and anxiety. But more than that, it was my acceptance of the beautiful invitation to celebrate the journey, even when the outcome was not yet known or had not yet arrived.

> Even when the world declines it, celebrate! Never turn down a good rescue, and never turn down an opportunity to celebrate.

Every mundane moment, even the undesirable ones, lead to the ultimate outcome: the salvation of our souls and ultimate glory in heaven. Never turn down a good rescue, and never turn down an opportunity to celebrate, rejoice, and place hope in that which is still on the way.

13

It's All In The Manure

My mother grew up on a large farm. I grew up with a large farm right behind my house in Waxhaw, NC. As a result, smelling cow patties, stepping in cow patties, avoiding cow patties, cleaning cow patties off my shoes, swatting flies from cow patties, throwing dried cow patties at friends, and anything else you could imagine about cow patties was familiar to me. There is nothing pleasing about manure from any kind of animal, yet any farmer or gardener will tell you they wouldn't waste an ounce of it.

It's true. That dark, rich soil that people lay down in their flower beds and vegetable gardens during spring begins with the dung from a herd of cows. Not that I'm an expert, but you basically pile up the manure, cover it with plastic, let it bake in the sun, take off the plastic, turn it over and over, work the soil, and repeat the process until you have the nutrient-rich soil. The process where the sun bakes through the plastic is what creates the nutrients for the soil. This process is called composting.

So let's review: stinky, unpleasant animal dung + persevering work of composting = nutrient-rich soil = luscious, great-tasting tomatoes and beautiful flowers. So, in essence, that grand tomato on your great-tasting BLT can trace its roots back to the nasty-smelling stuff coming out of the back of a cow.

When you're picking up and shoveling nasty manure in the hot sun, you can't see the beautiful flower or luscious tomato it will produce, at least not yet. When you're going through the not-so-pleasant process of composting manure, you have to fix your eyes on that which you can't yet see: the flower and the tomato. You can't see it yet, but you know if you go through the process, something beautiful will grow out of it. That's what enables you to get through the process. You don't get one without the other.

The most valued things always grow out of the most difficult things. That is why I believe that for those who place their trust in Christ, resurrection and eternal life are definite realities. They have a direct relationship with the valley of the shadow of death and suffering. 2 Corinthians 4:17-18 (NIV) says, "For our light and momentary troubles are achieving for us an eternal glory that far outweighs them all. So we fix our eyes not on what is seen, but on what is unseen, since what is seen is temporary, but what is unseen is eternal."

> The most valued things always grow out of the most difficult things.

Life is filled with not-so-pleasant, stinky moments we would all like to avoid if given the choice. Things like death, sickness, and suffering are not at the top of anyone's "favorite things to do" list. But they are realities of life, and the Scriptures promise we will go through them. The crucifixion was history's worst moment, and Jesus endured it for our sakes because of His love for us, thereby reconciling us to God. Jesus also defeated sin and death through the cross and resurrection. That was history's best moment! The glory of the resurrection was forged in the pain and suffering of the cross. The Bible calls that Good News!

Life is filled with difficult moments, but the Bible says those difficult moments are doing something. Every difficult moment we go through is "achieving for us an eternal glory that far outweighs" every ounce of death and suffering. It may not feel like it when we're going through it, but we have to keep our eyes on what we can't yet see. When it hurts so bad we can't seem to lift our heads, we must keep looking at the glory, the part we can't yet see but know is coming. Keep your eyes on the glory that the hard times are producing. The glory to come "far outweighs" all the suffering and death we experience in this temporary life on earth.

> For our light and momentary troubles are achieving for us an eternal glory that far outweighs them all. So we fix our eyes not on what is seen, but on what is unseen, since what is seen is temporary, but what is unseen is eternal.
>
> 2 CORINTHIANS 4:17-18

Just like the flower and the tomato in the compost, keep your eyes on the glory. The brilliance of glory is always around life's darkest corner. Light always shines in darkness! Life always triumphs over death! But understand this: it does so not because glory is a reward for suffering. It does so because glory is what grows out of suffering. The two are related, and you don't get one without the other. This is what gives the trials and suffering their meaning. It is the profound answer to the question we ask so often: "Why, Lord?" We don't always understand the reasons. It doesn't always make sense. But it is not for us yet to know all of the reasons and answers. It is for us to trust by faith. That is the part of the process we call sanctification.

God sits in glory, and He is preparing a glory for us so spectacular that our finite minds can barely imagine it. It doesn't feel that way in the process, but we must know that it is coming, and in the end, it will be more than worth it. He did it with the cross and resurrection, and He will do it again.

Sin, death, and hell have been conquered forever. Pain and suffering have their role in the process. We are living on this planet for only a short while compared to the eternity to come. For believers in Christ Jesus, this world is preparing us for what is to come. Heaven is a reality. It is not some far-off, mythical place.

The resurrection is a reality. It is our great hope. But the resurrection is also a person. His name is Jesus Christ (John 11:25). Jesus has conquered sin and death forever because of the cross and resurrection. For those who place their trust in Him, Jesus will come again one day. He will reign forever, and His people will reign with Him in glory. Everything will be new and redeemed. God will ultimately bring good out of the suffering. He will bring beauty from the mess. He is composting the difficulty of our lives and working it into something more glorious than we could ever imagine. Keep working the soil; the glory is coming!

> The brilliance of glory is always around life's darkest corner. It is not for us yet to know all of the reasons and answers. It is for us to trust by faith.

14

Being Right vs.
Being In Relationship

The setting was as close to perfect as you could get, a sublime ambience of winsomeness. My wife and I had just celebrated the jubilation of marriage with over 600 of our friends and family. Just three days into our honeymoon, we were surrounded by warm, clear Caribbean waters, slight breezes, lush white sands, beautiful blue skies, all the food we could eat, and lovely, kind people serving our every whim. All seemed right in our world. More than that, we were on top of our world.

All of a sudden, seemingly out of nowhere, we came plummeting down from the top of that perch by nothing more than, dare I say it, a game of putt-putt. At the resort where we were staying, putt-putt was part of the package, and you could play as much as you could handle. After a couple of days of sun and sand, we gleefully decided to venture onto the putt-putt course. That's when the bottom fell out. Being that we were newlyweds and blissfully in love, we decided to play "for fun." But the setting was so perfect and my wife so beautiful that the putt-putt failed to capture my attention. I gave little attention to whether a ball was making it into a hole. Needless to say, after 18 fun-filled holes, I came up on the short end of the scorecard. Plainly put, I lost.

Though I typically don't like to lose, losing wasn't the problem for me that day. The problem was what happened immediately after the scorecard was tabulated. As soon as I announced the score, my wife launched into a swaggered posture of grandstanding that, up until this point in our relationship, I wasn't aware she possessed. To be fair, my wife was never an athlete growing up, so "talking junk" didn't come naturally to her. As far as she was concerned, it was all innocent and fun-loving. But for me, building much of my childhood and college years around sports and competition...Well, let's just say, "It was on!"

Sometimes, it's more important to keep the peace than keep the score. "Being One" is more often better than "Having Just Won."

That was my first of many mistakes that day. As usual, I let my competitive spirit get the best of me. I played it cool, gently and lovingly asking for a rematch. When she politely declined, opting for time on the beach together, I kicked into another gear. Before I knew it, the next words that flew out of my mouth were, "You won't beat me again, not if I really try. It won't even be close." That was the moment I unearthed a lifelong, deeply hidden competitive side of my wife that, even to this day, can turn a simple game of Connect Four into an all-out war. Even when our kids were small, we couldn't complete a full game of Candy Land as a family without tears, grandstanding, and a family altar call to repentance and restoration.

Naturally, my wife consented to a rematch. Right there, in the midst of the sublime, perfect setting of the tropics on the heels of a storybook wedding with my dazzling wife, my only focus became dismantling my wife's putt-putt swagger piece by piece and leaving her in the abyss of a crushing loss.

Sadly, I accomplished exactly what I set out to do. I focused; I concentrated; I won. It wasn't even close. You would think that was enough. But then, even though it was light-hearted and all in fun, I was fool enough to exhibit for her a real case of "talking junk" on the battlefield of competition. Before I knew it, on just the third day of our honeymoon, we were having our first fight as a married couple. Did I mention my foolishness yet? Oh yeah, in the sentence above. For emphasis, let me say it one more time: foolishness.

There are times when one must stand and not compromise.

I learned an important lesson that day: sometimes, it's more important to be in relationship than to be right. Sometimes, it's more important to keep the peace than keep the score. "Being One" is more often better than "Having Just Won."

Let me be clear, there are moments in life when it is more important to stand for what is right than to compromise principles. Wars have been fought and won, and lives have been preserved because nations and peoples have stood for what is right, refusing compromise and surrender. There are certain eternal, Scriptural truths in which believers should never compromise, even if it costs them a few relationships in this fleeting world. There are times when one must stand and not compromise, even unto the loss of relationships, or even death.

But in between those pivotal, epic moments, there are far more prevailing moments in ordinary life that call for give and take. Ephesians 4:3 (NLT) says it this way: "Make every effort to keep yourselves united in the Spirit, binding yourselves together with peace."

When you realize the beauty of not having to be right all the time but being in relationship, and when you realize the reward of keeping peace rather than keeping score, then you meet in the middle, cooperate, and become one. This is where you experience true freedom, and this is ultimately where you get the win.

When you deviate from this, you become nothing more than a slave to your own ego and sovereignty. You may win, you may even be right, but you won't be free. You'll either push yourself further into the misery of isolation, or even worse, you'll be so narrow-minded that you can only tolerate being surrounded by those who think like you. In this mindset you'll never be challenged to true surrender and self-denial. You won't learn how to think deeper and more humbly about your own convictions.

> Make every effort to keep yourselves united in the Spirit, binding yourselves together with peace.
>
> EPHESIANS 4:3

When it's said and done, in most of these general, day-to-day circumstances that turn life from page to page, maybe you'll be more right than those who oppose you. Maybe you'll have the upper hand or the "win" on the scorecard of every conflict or cultural, familial, political, or even church collision. But if it comes at the expense of relationship and building bridges together, then no one wins. It took a putt-putt game in the middle of paradise for me to learn that. Thank God that's all it took.

15

The Organ Loft

My mother played the piano and the organ. For many years, she was the organist for the church where I was raised and grew up worshiping with others. She played the organ with force and passion. It wasn't with force like you're forcing something against its will, but force with such great intent and passion that it becomes graceful and beautiful.

On many Sunday services, Mom would allow me to sit in the organ loft with her. I would sit low at her feet. I remember watching her panty-hosed legs and feet press against the organ pedals with great vigor and potency. Sometimes, she even let me press the pedals. Then, I would watch her upper body sway side to side, forward, then back, almost like a locomotive. Her robe would sway with fashion and poise. At times I was in awe. Many Sundays, my mom's organ playing was the most exciting thing in those old traditional services.

Sadly, I outgrew the place at my mother's feet in the organ loft. But I did not outgrow the lessons those moments taught me.

One Saturday morning, my mother was asked to play the organ at the local Waxhaw Woman's Club Pancake

Breakfast Fundraiser. I was a pre-teen, and child-like innocence was slowly edging out of my system. As I ate my pancakes and syrup with delight, something caught my eye and swiftly swiped the delight from my heart. I saw two girls mimicking the Bride of Frankenstein playing a haunted organ and laughing. Much to my horror, they were mimicking my mother as she played the organ, and their impression was spot on. I know those two girls meant nothing by it. They loved my mom and were just being teenagers, but my mom had become the object of their parody.

In the blink of an eye, the feelings of awe I once felt in that organ loft were replaced with shame and embarrassment. Sadly, I felt my mom was becoming a source of humiliation for herself and for me.

On the way home, I asked, "Mom, why do you have to play the organ that way? Why do you have to move around so much and make those faces when you play? Why can't you just be still, calm, quiet, and not move so much?"

She looked at me and very calmly and delightfully gave me an answer I was not prepared to receive. She said, "You know, honey, I guess it's just because that's the way I express my love and joy for the Lord. I'm so thankful for all He has done that it just comes out of me naturally. I don't even know I'm doing it. It's my passion for Him that drives me, and I wouldn't have it any other way."

I quickly replied, "Yeah, but what about what all those people think...even the ones making fun of you?"

Appropriately, she said, "Let them laugh and have their fun. They're not my audience anyway. Jesus is my audience." Perfect. It was an answer that nullified any further response.

Years later, my mom came out of the organ loft and began to worship from the pew with the rest of us. Our church's general tone of worship growing up was stoic and reserved. As the old saying goes, we were very much like the "frozen chosen." That was not the case with my mom. She sang with joy. She sang with a volume that matched her joy. She smiled when she sang. She moved and swayed with passion, the same way she did when she played the organ. At first, her passion unnerved us and caused the rest of my family to slide down the pew to distance ourselves from her.

By that time, I was in my late teens. One Sunday, I asked her, "Mom, why can't you calm it down a little?"

Her answer was the same as it was years earlier from the organ loft. "This is how I express my love and thanks for the Lord. I don't want to hold anything back from God. He deserves my praise, and we should be joyful about what God has done."

I replied, "But what will people think?"

> Jesus is my audience. I care more about what God thinks. He is the reason we worship.

She responded, "I certainly don't want to be a distraction to anyone, but I also want people to know I have the joy of the Lord in my heart. I care more about what God thinks. He is the reason we worship." I wanted that joy in my heart as well.

Now, as a pastor and worship leader, there are still Sunday mornings before I get up on stage to worship with a church of believers that I reflect on sitting in that organ loft as a child at my mother's feet—the hosed feet pounding the organ pads, the shoulders passionately swaying back and forth, the many faces of splendor across her cheeks, and the choir robe swaying across the organ seat over my arms. I pray, "Lord, help me worship with force today. Not with the force that makes people do something they don't want to do, but with the kind of force and passion that pleases You and inspires joy in others."

I've now spent almost half my life designing and leading worship services. I never asked my mom, the one-time worship organist, for advice in leading worship. I never had to. That's because she gave me something better than advice.

In that organ loft and on that church pew so many years ago, she gave me and the congregation around her a piece of herself. That was the best advice I ever received for any worship experience.

> She gave me something better than advice. She gave me a piece of herself.

But more than that, she gave all of herself to God in worship. She held nothing back. She sought God's pleasure and glory above all else. I never forgot it, and I want my life to be marked by the same thing.

> *"Therefore, I urge you, brothers and sisters, in view of God's mercy, to offer your bodies as a living sacrifice, holy and pleasing to God—this is your true and proper worship."*
>
> Romans 12:1 (NIV)

16

Along The Way

"One regular chicken Philly sub on wheat bread, along with one regular turkey breast and provolone sub on wheat bread. Sure, we'll make them both a meal." That's the way it started. With a little red-headed kid, wearing a hat and a sleeveless shirt, going to lunch at Jersey Mike's on a Saturday with his dad. A Saturday morning training session on the tennis court always preceded the lunch. The premise was that if my oldest son, Jadon, would hustle and try hard at the session, he would be rewarded with a free lunch at Jersey Mike's. I never told Jadon this, but the truth was that we were going to lunch either way after the session. Of course, I wanted Jadon to learn the game, but tennis was secondary. Spending time with my kid was the primary endeavor.

Those Saturday sessions seemed a bit arbitrary at the time, fading and blending in with all the other mundane moments of everyday life. While we were in those moments, they may have seemed incidental or random, sprinkled in with the normal rhythms of life. But unknown to us at the time, those little Saturday morning training sessions would become bigger than anything we intended or imagined. They were not meant to be the destination; they were not meant to be the point. However, they led to a destination unplanned and all that took place along the way.

The tendency in life is to think your journey is mostly random and mundane moments, with a little bit of epic sprinkled in to give life its spice and make it bearable. We tend to think life is made up mostly of mundane moments that serve to get us to something bigger or better, like working for the weekend.

For many of us, most of these unacknowledged moments take place during the five-day work week before the long-awaited weekend. But nothing could be further from the truth. Those little moments in between become key components of what lies ahead. Those along-the-way, arbitrary moments can actually become the moments we were meant for but haven't discovered yet. That is why it is so important to have the correct approach to every day we live and every moment that God gifts us.

> Those along-the-way, arbitrary moments can actually become the moments we were meant for but haven't discovered yet.

Your approach to life will either choke you into dysfunction, boredom, or misguided faith, or it will lead you into joy, expectant hope, and edifying faith. Much of this will depend upon how you approach what you believe to be the insignificant, mundane, and random moments of life.

I have come to the personal conviction, based on my own life experience, that nothing about life is insignificant or mundane. Our path is as important as the destination. Along-the-way moments have incredible potential if we stop and take notice.

In the Bible, in Luke 8:40-56 a man named Jairus came to Jesus, fell at his feet, and begged him to come home with him and heal his dying twelve-year-old daughter. Jesus went with him. Jesus had a destination and a goal. Jairus had a goal and destination. All paths led to the healing of Jairus' daughter. But something else profound happened along the way.

The story goes on to say that while Jesus was going "along the way" to Jarius' house to heal his daughter, a woman came up to him and grabbed the fringe of his robe. While surrounded by a crowd, Jesus immediately stopped everything and asked, "Who touched me?" His disciples responded, "Master, this whole crowd is pressing up against you." Essentially, "Jesus, you're in a crowd of people. Everyone is touching you!" True, but Jesus only noticed the touch of one. It was the touch of a desperate woman who needed something along-the-way. Jesus noticed the cry and urgency of her desperation.

> Jesus stopped for the along-the-way and then continued to the destination and goal.

I want my prayers to have that same kind of urgency, belief, and passion.

Jesus was on the way toward a destination, but He wasn't going to let this along-the-way moment pass or lose significance. When the woman realized she could no longer conceal her identity, she identified herself. The moment they locked eyes, Jesus told her, "Your faith has made you well. Go in peace." She was healed instantly. I bet she was glad she grabbed that along-the-way moment.

In the mean-time imagine Jairus standing there and thinking, *Jesus, we have a destination and a goal. My daughter is dying. We need to get going!* Jairus needed a goal and a destination. The bleeding woman needed an along-the-way. Both had value and to Jesus, both were important. He stopped for the along-the-way and then continued to the destination and goal.

Jesus eventually ended up at Jairus' house and healed his son as well. To Jairus, the destination meant everything.

To the woman healed while Jesus was on the journey, the along-the-way meant everything. Every moment has purpose, even when you think it doesn't and even when you don't see the big picture.

Now, back to chicken Philly subs on a Saturday.

I had a successful career in tennis from the time I was in high school, through college, and even to this day. I went to college on a tennis scholarship and became a tennis pro at a local swim and racquet club, teaching tennis to adults and their children. It was how I made a living my first summer after graduating college, along with being a high school tennis coach. Now, I am married, a father to three boys, and teaching the game to my own children.

However, I put a basketball in Jadon's hands long before a tennis racquet. Together, we've had many more basketball training sessions than tennis training sessions. It was no surprise that basketball was his passion, and that is where his dreams began to find their footing. The dream/destination/goal was to play college basketball, so tennis became secondary. Tennis was simply something I made Jadon play because he needed a second sport and it complemented the footwork and hand-eye coordination of basketball. He grew to love tennis, but basketball was and still is his passion.

In the years since Jadon was a young kid learning how to play tennis, I went from being a dad teaching tennis and basketball to his kids and supplying them with subs, back to being a high school tennis coach in 2022. This time, I was serving as the coach to my son Jadon, who was now a senior in high school, and to my middle son, Ryder, who was a freshman in high school.

Those Saturday morning tennis sessions were now a distant, pleasant memory. Jadon had already achieved his dream and accepted an offer to play college basketball on the heels of winning Conference Player of the Year in basketball his senior year. The journey seemed to be on course.

The goal and the destination were coming into full view, and we were still building on that dream.

But before we knew it, along-the-way found its way into our lives. Jadon won Conference Player of the Year in tennis his senior year as well. Jadon also went undefeated in the singles competition, and he and his partner won the conference title in doubles and were now playing in the finals for the Regional Doubles Championship! We'd come a long way from the little sleeveless kid hitting tennis balls just to earn a sub at Jersey Mike's.

It was the Finals of the Regional Championships. Everything was on the line. A successful and unexpected season had led to this pressure-filled moment. The air was thick with anticipation and excitement. After a hard-fought match, Jadon and his partner dominated their opponents. It was now match point for Jadon and his partner, and I stood to my feet, along with the rest of the crowd. As I waited in excited anticipation for the next point, I briefly thought, *How did we get here, and how did it happen so fast?* Basketball was still the destination. It was the goal. Yet, here we were along-the-way, playing for a championship in another sport.

The opponents served. Jadon swung his racquet for a booming forehand. Winner! Elation! Jadon and his partner were the Regional Champions! Then it happened. Jadon immediately looked up at me, gave me the biggest smile, and held up his fist. The moment we locked eyes, everything around me froze in time. It was as if Jadon and I were the only two people in the universe. It seemed as if I was immediately catapulted back to those moments on the court on Saturday morning and lunch at Jersey Mike's. I would have never thought those moments would one day lead us to this moment of joy and gladness, but they did. It all happened along the way to something else. I wouldn't trade it for anything.

As Jadon and his partner accepted their championship medals on the court, the reality set in for me. None of this was the destination. Basketball was the destination, not tennis. All of this just happened along-the-way, and yet, it seemed to fall into place so perfectly. Nothing was random about those Saturday mornings, even if we had never won any championships. It was one dad and one kid making the most of the time they had together.

I never dreamed about being a tennis coach. I never even dreamed about being a father or a pastor. I was supposed to follow a dream of getting a record deal and going to Hollywood to act when I got out of college. Nothing about my life or choices would have seemed to lead to where I am now, but it all happened along-the-way. It almost seems as though the most significant parts of my life have hap-

Sometimes, the thing you want most in life is right beside you all along.

pened along-the-way to something else I thought I was sup- posed to be doing. Sometimes, the thing you want most in life is right beside you all along, but you fail to see it be- cause you are so preoccupied with something that seems bigger or better.

I don't know where Jadon's destination will lead with basketball, or tennis, for that matter. We are simply taking it step by step and enjoying the journey. Even at an age where most people say that I should discard any dreams I may have, I refuse. I still feel like God has more for me. Regardless of where we end up, I have discovered that life is filled with some pretty incredible moments in the along- the-way of every day. Whether those moments are leading to the destination, or are, in fact, the destination themselves, matters not to me. That is the miracle of the mundane, the random, the small, the in-between, or the destination itself. They all have their own beauty and are worthy of discovery.

I don't need it to be "5 o'clock somewhere." There's just as much beauty and wonder in the 3 o'clock right here in front of me. I don't need to travel somewhere else to be in my happy place. I am surrounded by happy places each day that I draw air in my lungs. Each moment has incredible potential, regardless of my geographical location and what path I may be on at the time.

I've discovered that I need a goal and a destination, but I also need an along-the-way. Both have incredible value and hold something special. Whether we need an along-the-way moment like the bleeding woman or a destination like Jairus, Jesus is compassionate and interested enough to make room for both and use them in a wonderful way. I learned that along the way to another destination, and I'm not done yet.

17

Prayer

It was the night of January 3, 2017. A night that, for good or bad, will forever be engraved on my memories. It was a routine night like any other until this point of our lives. Suddenly, breaking through the silence of bedtime preparation, I heard my wife screaming my name and yelling, "There's something wrong with Ryder! There's something wrong with Ryder!" This kind of urgent yell immediately grabs your attention and sends your heart crashing full throttle into your stomach. I ran down the hall to Ryder's bedroom to find our middle son in a full-blown seizure, shaking, murmuring, and lying face down on his bed.

I am aware that for many who deal with seizures regularly, they can be quite common and chronic. But as common as they may be to some, they are never routine or without effect. For many others, they can be deadly. At the onset of Ryder's seizure, my mind immediately went to friends of ours whose little girl had a seizure on the playground at school many years earlier. Tragically, their daughter never woke up or came out of that seizure, and she died that day in the middle of a playground surrounded by children.

While my wife dialed 911, all I knew to do was roll my son on his side, lay beside him, and hold him. Frantically,

I prayed over and over, "Jesus, help! God, please don't take my son." As I prayed these words, my mind was distraught over the fact that they were even coming out of my mouth. I had been in emergency situations before, but none this personal. I had prayed for many others who had been in similar situations, but I was in shock that such trauma had found its way to our doorstep.

Theologically speaking, I knew that God would never simply "take my son" in some act of cruel sovereignty that I would never be able to explain or accept. I knew our world, in all forms, is broken. I knew that tragedy happens because of that brokenness. I also knew that, while God doesn't necessarily always bring these tragedies into our lives, He won't waste them either. He will use them to bring about His purpose, draw us nearer to Him, make us stronger and more aware of His grace, and give deeper meaning to eternity and living life with an eternal perspective while here on earth.

> I also knew that, while God doesn't necessarily always bring these tragedies into our lives, He won't waste them either.

But in moments like this, proper theology isn't always running with the timeline of trauma. All I knew to do was pray to God, who had always been faithful and never abandoned me. I had stood by many bedsides and prayed with those who were dying and their families, but at that moment, the only words I could muster were, "Jesus, help! God, please don't take my son." Whether they were appropriate at the moment I could not know; they were words simply born out of a relationship with a Heavenly Father that I knew loved me and was an "ever-present help in time of trouble" (Psalm 46:1-NIV).

While my mouth was verbalizing those words, unbelievably, my mind was in the same moment, fast-forwarding to what life would be like without Ryder. While I was praying, "God, don't take my son," I was thinking, *If You do, please show us how to live without him and move forward while still being faithful to You.* It was no doubt one of the most desperate prayers I have ever prayed. It seemed as though every sensory in my brain and spirit was going off at the same time.

Thankfully, the medics arrived, and Ryder slowly came out of the seizure. As I traveled down the road with him in that ambulance to the emergency room, he began to talk. As he began to talk, my heart rate began to slow, and my breath normalized. The sound of his voice quickly became the sweetest sound I had ever heard. It made me realize how much we take for granted the sound of those voices we hold dearest. I decided I would never take those voices for granted again. I decided I would never assume a posture of irritability with their laughs, screams, cries, or questions, no matter how tired I was or what kind of day I was having.

> It dawned on me that the things I saw as an irritant or that may have been hard were actually blessings.

The next few months would be filled with doctor's visits and tests. At the end of that journey, after months of tests and prodding, Ryder was given clearance from the doctors and was able to resume a healthy life and return to normal activities.

The years following that seizure would include the life-jarring transition into adulthood. Not long after, Ryder journeyed into adolescence. That sweet little voice that comforted me in the ambulance now grew much deeper. We stored away old toys and outgrown clothes. Social media, cell phones, and computers replaced action figures, toy trains, toy cars, and Lego blocks. Toilet seats and bathroom floors were stained much more frequently, and Ryder began to emit a certain teen odor that wasn't all that pleasant. Rubber bands from braces were left on bathroom sinks, and food was eaten at a rate faster than our wallets could compete.

It was absolutely jarring to me the day we had to buy a razor to maintain the facial hair on his face. As if that wasn't enough, we were now getting a driver's license and buying a car for Ryder. As overwhelming as it all was, my heart sank completely when, only weeks after we joyously surprised him with that new car on Christmas Day, we were confronted with the crushing expense of a brand new engine for that same car. We didn't have the money for that engine, but we found a way.

Being a former youth pastor, I'm fully aware of these changes and stages of life and the progression of adolescence through the teen years.

Every moment is now a gift—even the hard ones.

But through the experiences of my own children, I am learning that the process is completely different when it's your own kids and your own life. Watching all my kids grow older and into their own has been a joyful and satisfying experience, but it has also been more difficult than I would have ever imagined. I have had to grieve the loss of their childhood. For the most part, I have not grieved in a way that has not been able to let go and let them grow, but more in a way that has just been thankful that we got to do every moment. I am thankful for each stage, but I will always miss those "little kid" days.

Amid this journey into adulthood with Ryder, something beautiful also took place in the life-jarring moments of growth and transition. Every single one of these moments of transition was connected to a prayer I had prayed over Ryder in one of my life's most traumatic moments just years earlier. I realized every single puberty-driven, irritating, adolescent thing that Ryder did was an answer to prayer.

Every urine stain, every rubber band I picked up that came off his braces, every grocery bill, every crumb I picked up, every empty cookie box or bag of chips, and yes, even the new engine we didn't expect to pay for—all of it was an answer to a prayer I had prayed on the night of January 3, 2017.

Every tear, every transition, every dollar, every ounce of body odor, every single thing that I labored through with him, everything I had found irritating and hard to process— every single part was an answer to that desperate prayer, "Jesus, help! God, please don't take my son." It dawned on me that the things I saw as an irritant or that may have been hard were actually blessings. All of these so-called struggles were actually an answer to prayer. God saved my son's life that night, and Ryder was still with us.

> The primary purpose of prayer is not always to change my circumstances but to change and mold me to God's will in the midst of my circumstances.

Even amid his junior season of high school basketball, I was frustrated with his lack of playing time and opportunity on the court to get better. I was frustrated that he wasn't utilized the right way and given opportunities for his talent and skill to help make the team better. I was frustrated that all of the work we had put in up until this point didn't seem to be coming to fruition the way I had planned. I did not see things the way his coach saw them. These were frustrations for Ryder, my wife, and me. But as much as it wasn't turning the way I wanted it to, the hard parts were still answers to a prayer I had prayed almost seven years prior to that season: "Jesus, help! God, please don't take my son." Ryder was still here, and even in the frustrating moments that gave us opportunities to grow, the faithfulness of God's answer to my prayer was greater than any amount of playing time. He was still in the battle.

Everything that happens with Ryder from this moment on will always be connected to that desperate prayer that I prayed in a traumatic moment. The realization of this wonderful fact changes my view and posture toward everything. Every moment is now a gift—even the hard ones. God's kindness is such that we should not take the hard or the miniscule for granted, particularly when He sent them to us as a blessing we weren't expecting.

In the Bible, Revelation 5:8 (ESV) says that in heaven, when everyone gathers to worship before Jesus, there will be "golden bowls full of incense, which are the prayers of the saints." When God brings everything to its epic conclusion, the prayers of the faithful will play a significant role.

> Never stop praying. Be thankful in all circumstances, for this is God's will for you who belong to Christ Jesus.
>
> 1 THESSALONIANS 5:17-18

There are greater theological ramifications to discuss with regard to prayer. However, as it pertains to this conversation, this passage tells me every prayer I've ever prayed, and every prayer I ever will pray, matters and is doing something eternally that is beyond my finite comprehension. None of my prayers are without effect or random. They all matter, even when I don't see or feel it. Somehow, in God's eternal plan for history, our prayers are counting for something far beyond what we can imagine, and they are all linked together in His glorious story. What a grand thought and motivation for prayer!

I know that every prayer I pray will not always get answered the way I pray it. My prayer for Ryder the night of his seizure could have gone the other way, and it has for many who prayed the same way. But I've come to realize that the primary purpose of prayer is not always to change my circumstances but to change and mold me to God's will in the midst of my circumstances, whatever they may be or however they may unfold in His plan for my life.

My prayers, as simple as they may seem, as theologically incompetent as they may feel, all have more far-reaching effects than I can imagine. I pray simply because it is God's will for my life. 1 Thessalonians 5:17-18 (NLT) tells us, "Never stop praying. Be thankful in all circumstances, for this is God's will for you who belong to Christ Jesus."

> The Holy Spirit helps us in our weakness. For example, we don't know what God wants us to pray for. But the Holy Spirit prays for us... And the Father who knows all hearts knows what the Spirit is saying, for the Spirit pleads for us believers in harmony with God's own will.
>
> ROMANS 8:26-27

But I also pray with a Helper. For the believer, the Helper is God's Holy Spirit. The Scriptures say in Romans 8:26-27 (NLT), "the Holy Spirit helps us in our weakness. For example, we don't know what God wants us to pray for. But the Holy Spirit prays for us...And the Father who knows all hearts knows what the Spirit is saying, for the Spirit pleads for us believers in harmony with God's own will."

Amazing! Even when I don't know how to put the words together for my prayer, God's Spirit picks up at my weakness and prays on my behalf, praying a prayer that puts me in harmony with God's will. There is power in trusting that fact! Every prayer is worth the effort, even when we don't know what to say. Even when it may feel like jumbled words, God's Spirit can pick it up and work it for something greater than we could have ever done at the start.

I am left with many conclusions and questions. Are there things in my life that I currently see as irritations that could in fact be some of the Lord's greatest blessings? How would this change my perspective?

Perhaps my body aches more than it once did. But perhaps that's a reminder that God has brought me through a lot of difficulty, and I'm still here. Maybe my life seems more complicated these days, but perhaps I'm being trusted with more opportunities to get better through those complications. Perhaps all those crumbs I'm constantly sweeping off the kitchen counter are a reminder that my pantry is still full of food, when much of the world goes hungry. Perhaps the house I can never seem to keep clean enough is a reminder that I have a roof over my head. Perhaps the toys I'm constantly stepping over are a reminder that a family surrounds me. Perhaps the grief that seems to be overwhelming me is an opportunity to press into God, who is preparing for me

> Every prayer is worth the effort, even when we don't know what to say. Every prayer will find its place in the perfect ending that God has for each of us.

an eternity that far outweighs all my current struggles and grief. Perhaps this will develop a sense of hope that is deeper than anything I've ever experienced. Perhaps the graveside I'm standing beside is a reminder that death is not the end, nor does it have the final say in our lives. Perhaps my current failure is an opportunity to get back up. The list is endless, but will I be open to seeing these unseen blessings? It seems as though God gives that choice to us.

The night of Ryder's seizure ended in an emergency room. But as the clock struck 12:01 a.m. in that ER, the next day began with us surrounded by friends and family who had driven long miles in the middle of the night to sit with us and remind us that we were loved and not alone.

I would prefer another way to be reminded that I am loved and not alone, but God used this one, and it had an impact.

Every day with Ryder—the good, the bad, the difficult, and the easy—is littered with answers to a desperate prayer that I prayed on January 3, 2017, in one of the most traumatic moments of my life. These moments will be forever connected, and my outlook will forever be changed on this side of heaven.

Amazingly, those are just the parts of my prayers that I see with my limited and finite sight here on earth. One can only imagine what awaits or arises from those prayers in eternity one day. I see with only limited vision this side of heaven. I only see this small version of the big picture. But the Scriptures tell me in eternity, my limited vision will cease; all things will come into perfect vision and make sense. 1 Corinthians 13:12a (NLT) says, "Now we see things imperfectly, like puzzling reflections in a mirror, but then we will see everything with perfect clarity."

> Now we see things imperfectly, like puzzling reflections in a mirror, but then we will see everything with perfect clarity.
>
> 1 CORINTHIANS 13:12A

Oh, the wonder of seeing God's perfect plan come to fullness and perfection. Until then, my task is to remain faithful, believe, trust, and keep praying and hoping.

So, let us pray without ceasing. The simple, the desperate, the hard, the wordless, the joyful, the tear-filled, the senseless—every single prayer matters; every prayer is always doing something. We are constantly being changed. We are constantly walking, surrounded by wonder and blessing. Every prayer is filled with opportunities for faith and hope. Every prayer will find its place in the perfect ending that God has for each of us. So, let us pray.

18
Coming Home

My goodbye letter had been hand-written with pencil on a piece of notebook paper. I thanked my parents for everything but informed them that I didn't want to disappoint them anymore. This would be the last time they would see me. I was leaving home and running away, and, hopefully, we would all be better for it. I left the letter on the kitchen table.

I had packed about enough snacks to make it through one afternoon and one change of clothes. I slung the bag over my shoulders, mounted my bicycle, and made my way down the road in front of our house, going who knows where. I hadn't planned that far yet. It was more about where I was leaving than where I was going. This was the end; I was running away from home. I was ten years old.

My reason for leaving home was quite miniscule in the grand scheme of things, but to me on that day, it was the only thing that mattered. Report cards were coming out. Once again, my grades would be below average. I wasn't a below average student. It was just that my effort pertaining to my studies and school work was below average.

I had been more interested in sports and recreation than grades and schoolwork up until this point in my life. My parents did not share my philosophy, which is where the conflict ensued. Being a former school teacher, my mother did not share my lack of enthusiasm toward schoolwork. This would be another average report card, another disappointment, and another grounding for a period of time.

The problem was that I began to equate my value and worth with my grades, report card, and performance in school. Truthfully, my parents never asked for perfection when it came to grades and report cards. They just asked for effort, but it took me a while before that caught on. I actually began to apply myself to learning the closer I got to receiving an athletic scholarship to college.

But in this stage of my life, I mistakenly attached my value to my performance in school. I was fearful of another punishment and another round of disappointment for my parents. Feeling I would never be able to meet any perceived expectations and that I was letting everyone down, I decided to give up and check out.

> To your Heavenly Father, you have great value.

Sadly, there are many who feel they'll never be able to live up to expectations. There are many who feel they can't bear another round of disappointment, so they decide to leave and give up on their families. There are those who feel they can't bear another dose of failure or defeat and decide to check out of life.

I assure you, no matter how crushing your defeat or failure may feel, no matter how disappointing your life may seem right now, no matter how valueless you may feel, nothing could be further from the truth. To your Heavenly Father, you have great value, so much value that He gave up His life and rose again for you. In His life, your life finds its meaning and purpose. He will never abandon or give up on you, even when it seems like everyone else has given up.

You are always worth it, no matter what you have done or what you have failed to do.

There is a story in the Bible in Luke 15:11-32 that Jesus shared, giving us a true snapshot of the Father's love for us. We know this story as "The Prodigal Son" or "The Lost Son," but we could just as well call it "The Loving, Forgiving Father Who Never Gives Up On Us."

In this story a young son decided to leave home to strike out on his own and make a name for himself. He wanted his own independence and to experience all that life had to offer. He came to his father and asked for his share of the estate.

From a Middle Eastern perspective, the inheritance meant the life and legacy of the father to the family. But the son didn't ask for the inheritance. He was careful to ask for his share, his piece, what was coming to him. In this instance, he was thinking only of himself and his future; he had no thought or care for carrying on the legacy of his father or his family. He only wanted his share for his life, without any accountability to anyone else. It was an insult to the father and the family to ask for such a thing before the death of the father, but that did not stop the son from asking for his share.

We can treat God our Father the same way at times. We're not concerned with His glory or His will for our lives. We just want Him to give us blessings without accountability and responsibility so that we can live our lives on our terms and not His terms. When we do this, it never works out as planned. It's always a disastrous end.

In this story, the father gave his son his share. This is the picture of God letting the sinner go his or her own way. The Lord gives us freewill to make our own choices because He wants our following Him to be rooted in love and sacrifice rather than be built upon what we are going to get out of the transaction, as human nature is so prone to do.

Fittingly, choosing to rebel and go his own way, the boy squandered all of his wealth and ended up literally eating with pigs. This is always where sin and rebellion leave us. It promises great things and gives temporary, short-term pleasure, but in the end, it leaves us in the mud, in misery, with the pigs.

After finding himself neck-deep in the shame and guilt of his own sin and rebellion, starving and lonely, the son came to the end of himself and wanted to go back home in repentance. Repentance is a privilege. It is always the first step to a changed life and coming back home to freedom, where we belong with the Father.

The issue with coming home was that the son knew in the current culture, the father's expected response would be to slap his son in the face with anger. He would slap him with the backside of his left hand, as this would be more degrading than the open palm of the right hand. This was meant to express humiliation and disappointment. It would be done publicly.

So, the son crafted a plan to ask his father to be a hired servant so he could pay the money back and get back in good standing with the father. With this plan in mind, he headed back home.

Many of us serve God this way. We realize we have made a poor decision, or perhaps we've made a lifestyle of poor and destructive decisions. To get back in good standing with God, who we presume wants to beat us down, we craft a plan that if we can do enough good things, we'll somehow make up for all the bad things we've done. We believe if we manage to pull this off, it will somehow even out the scale and make God love us again.

The son began to make his way home with his plan in mind. As he walked, he was fully aware of what was to come when he arrived. Any Jew who loses money among foreigners faces the *Kezazah,* which means "cutting off." He would be cut off from the family, symbolically represented by breaking a clay pot at his feet. This would be done publicly and was designed to show that the community rejected him forever. He would live as a slave among them rather than as a son.

When the son was within eye distance of the house, he looked to the top of the hill and saw his father standing there, looking in his direction. Unknown to the son at the time was that the father had been standing there looking, waiting, praying, and hoping that his son would return home since the day he left. He never gave up on him.

You are never so far that God can't reach you. It's never too late for you to start over.

It was here that the most amazing part took place. The father began to run toward his son. In this culture, it would be considered humiliating for men over 40 years of age to run, yet this father sprinted toward his son.

Perhaps at this point, the son was so overwhelmed with fear that he thought anger was driving his father toward him, that the punishment was about to be dispensed with great fury. But it was the opposite; it was love and compassion that drove this father to do what no other man in the culture did.

Notice in v.20 of this passage, it states, "And while he was still a long way off, his father saw him coming. Filled with love and compassion, he ran to his son, embraced him, and kissed him" (NLT).

You may feel like you are a "long way off" from God right now. But amazingly, we have a God who specializes in the "long way off." You are never so far that God can't reach you. Your situation is never so far gone that God can't change it. You are never so deep that God can't pull you out. All you need is the courage and faith to take a step toward Him. As you do, be overwhelmed by the love of the Heavenly Father, who will run toward you and embrace you with a love and compassion like you have never felt. It's never too late, and you're never too far gone to come home. It's never too late for you to start over.

Fittingly, in verse 21, the young rebel said, "Father, I have sinned against both heaven and you, and I am no longer worthy of being called your son." The father draped his arms around his son and embraced him. There was no talk of the boy's rebellion because the father knew his son was repentant and had taken responsibility for his actions.

When we take the wrong course and make selfish, sinful decisions, we must take responsibility and own our stuff. God has given us repentance as a gift and privilege. Never be ashamed to receive that gift and use it. It is the very thing that will lead to a fresh start and a new beginning.

> Every course that begins with surrender to God always changes from disappointment to celebration.

Verses 22-23 go on to say, "But his father said to the servants, 'Quick! Bring the finest robe in the house and put it on him. Get a ring for his finger and sandals for his feet. And kill the calf we have been fattening. We must celebrate with a feast, for this son of mine was dead and has now returned to life. He was lost, but now he is found.' So the party began."

There was only love and celebration. The son realized his only task was not to try and earn his way back but to simply accept being found again. The son was satisfied to be a slave, but the father restored him to full son-ship and membership back into the family.

God does the same with all who call on Him in repentance. Every course that begins with surrender to God always changes from disappointment to celebration. It's never too late to come home.

Ten years old and with a bag on my back, I peddled as fast as I could away from my house. I was leaving behind all the perceived disappointment and fear. I was running away from home. But I was also running away from my problems rather than facing them as I should. It's amazing how the Enemy will make you feel that running away from your problems is the best course of action. We should not be surprised by such acts from a devil whose only goal is to "steal, kill, and destroy" (John 10:10).

I managed to make it a full three blocks from my house when I suddenly realized, "I don't know where I'm going or have any place to go." I took a hard left turn down to the pond behind my aunt's house. There was a pond in the woods surrounded by trees. I would be safely hidden until I figured things out.

> The first step to the turnaround is always the hardest.

One hour went by, then another hour, and another. Before long it was afternoon. I had eaten all of my snacks and began to get hungry again. I had no money. The reality of what I had done began to hit my young heart. I was only three blocks from home, but it felt like 3,000 miles.

Just then, I began to see the town's only police cars and a few of the county deputy police cars scouring the neighborhood and the town. I saw my mother and father's cars riding back in forth through town. I could hear the faint screams of neighbors calling my name in the distance. They were all looking for the kid who ran away from home and all the disappointment. They were looking for me.

I began to cry. I wanted to go home. I wanted my mommy and daddy. I wanted someone to hug me and tell me it was going to be okay. But I didn't know how. I was too ashamed and too undone.

For a moment I thought, *If I go back, the punishment will be worse. My parents will punish me, the police will punish*

123

me, and the neighbors will reject me for disrupting their day. I can't go back. I will be humiliated. Those thoughts were coming from an Enemy who wanted to isolate me and make me feel like I couldn't go home.

The thought then occurred to me. *Someone is looking for me. Maybe, just maybe, I do have value. Maybe there is someone who cares. Maybe I can go home and start over.*

Understand this: no matter how far you go, no matter how bad things may seem, there is always someone thinking about you who cares. That someone is your Heavenly Father, the One who created you "fearfully and wonderfully" (Psalm 139:14). You can always come home and start over. God loves you and He will never abandon you.

> Life is worth the living, and disappointments can lead to life's greatest victories if we keep getting back up.

As hard as it was, through tears, fear, and a lot of doubt, I managed to pick up my bicycle and start pushing it up the hill, out of the woods, across the field, and toward the road that led home. I knew as soon as I hit the top of that hill, I would be in full view of everyone who was looking for me. There would be no turning back.

But I also knew it was time to stop hiding and running. That would be the first step to a turnaround and a new start. The first step to the turnaround is always the hardest. But in the end, every tear, every stain, and every step is worth it.

I crested the hill. Just as I did, I looked off in the distance and saw my mom down at the bottom of the hill looking for me. My father wasn't far behind. He was sweating, standing in the middle of the road in the hot afternoon sun, fully dressed in a suit and tie from his work at the bank. I knew if he had left work in the middle of the day to drive all the way home just to look for me, it had to be serious. Was it anger and disappointment that drove him home? No, it was love.

When my mom turned and saw me, she began to sprint up the hill toward me. I dropped my bicycle and my bag to the ground and just stood there sobbing. By the time she got to me, she was weeping. She wrapped her arms around me and hugged me. We both stood there crying. There were no words.

The neighbors and the police smiled and soon went on their way, back to the rhythm of their day before it had been abruptly interrupted by the kid who ran away from home.

> Grace is always a greater motivator than anything else.

My dad picked my bike up off the street and put my bag over his shoulder. By now, he had sweat through his suit from work. Few words were spoken. There was only love, only compassion. Together, we walked the remaining two blocks back home. We sat at the kitchen table and had cookies and milk together. It was a moment worthy of a celebration. A lost son had been found.

That day, I learned that no matter how much you try, you can't run from your problems. Sooner or later, the right thing to do is to turn around and face them, no matter how hard it may seem. I learned that the first step to the turn-around is owning your own stuff and repenting. It won't be easy, especially not at first, but it will be well worth it in the end.

I learned that no matter how far you go, no matter how much you mess up, you're never so far gone that you can't come home. I learned there is always someone who loves you, even if that only person is your Heavenly Father. Life is worth the living, and disappointments can lead to life's greatest victories if we keep getting back up.

My parents learned that people will mess up and make mistakes, especially children. Not every expectation will be met. There will be disappointment and struggle. But everyone needs a second chance and a lot of mercy and grace. They learned that while punishment and consequences have their place in life, grace is always a greater motivator than anything else.

The pond and the woods where I hid that day have long since been paved over by apartments, but the intersection where I hugged my parents is still there. My childhood home and the road we walked to get home is still there in Waxhaw, NC. I still think of that day, that journey, and the lessons learned quite often when I go back to visit my parents in my old hometown.

> Repentance is a privilege. Own your stuff. Face your problems.

I've had to make that spiritual journey many times over the course of my life. My selfishness and rebellion have left me at the bottom of many a hill, wanting to hide from God and my own problems. But each time, I come back to the same lessons I learned that day.

Repentance is a privilege. Own your stuff. Face your problems. Get up and take the first step. It won't be easy, but when you do, at the top or bottom of every hill, you'll always find a Heavenly Father waiting with arms wide open, who never gave up on you. He will come running to you every time and embrace you with compassion. You matter. You are not a disappointment. Your life has meaning. The turnaround is just around the corner. You're never too far gone, and it's never too late to come home.

Honoring the Fallen

19

Toy Soldiers

A story I wrote to honor the fallen.

You could buy a bag of 48 toy soldiers for $3.99. Accessories, toy tanks, and jets were sold separately. If you saved up enough, you could assemble quite the battle on a tabletop or in the dirt. The soldiers came in different forms and positions and carried different weapons—some crawled, some stood, some ran, and others shouted orders. What struck me most about my toy soldiers was that their faces always bore the angst and agony of battle—every single one of them.

A few of the boys in town always gathered down at Mr. Horn's General Store to play with our toy soldiers. He had the best dirt out back to stage our epic battles. On a good day or when it wasn't busy, Mr. Horn would clear off a table inside and let us stage the toy soldier battle there. We felt bigger inside because that's where the old men of the town hung around. Many had served in the Armed Forces and fought in the Great War.

On the rare occasion, a few would even offer strategies to our make-believe scenarios and position the soldiers more fittingly to accomplish the mission. If we were really lucky, we might even get a story out of it. But the stories rarely had a conclusion. That's because the former soldiers telling them usually quivered at the lip and buckled under the weight of the tears flowing from their eyes. The hand of a fellow veteran would quickly appear upon his shoulder, and he would excuse himself from the scene. The silence in those moments was deafening and awkward. It didn't seem decent to keep moving the toy soldiers about when the re-al-life soldiers in front of us were struggling with the horrors of the things we made up for recreation. So, we would slowly and quietly pack up all our toy soldiers, tanks, and guns.

Each time we packed up the soldiers, without fail, Mr. Horn would always come over and say, "Now, boys, get all those soldiers in the bag. You make sure you never leave any soldier behind. I don't care how wounded or maimed they may be; you bring them home!" He always seemed to say it with emotion, force, and sometimes a few tears. Then, he would count my bag with scrutiny to make sure I had all 48 with me. "All of them go home!" he said.

For a while, we didn't understand; we thought we were just picking up toy soldiers. If we lost any, we could always go to the store and buy more. But Mr. Horn always made sure we left none behind or lost them. We had a few get chewed by the dogs or lose a limb due to getting stepped on. Mr. Horn took pleasure in melting down the wounded parts and fusing them back together, or applying duct tape for a quick fix. He would say, "Every one of these soldiers has someone who loves them and is praying for them to come home. You make sure you fix them up and take care of them." To us, they were just lifeless plastic trinkets, but to Mr. Horn, they represented so much more.

My daddy grew up with Mr. Horn's son, Jimmy, and spent a lot of time in the Horn house as a child and teenag-er. One day, I asked him about Mr. Horn's devotion to our toy soldiers. I had seen the picture of Jimmy Horn many times. It hung in the center of his father's general store. He was dressed in military uniform. Beside it was a photo of Mr. Horn with his arm around his son one day after they went fishing. I always figured Jimmy was off serving somewhere as a high-ranking officer in the military, and that's why we never saw him. That would also explain why his father was so passionate about how we cared for our toy soldiers. That's when my daddy told me, "Son, Jimmy Horn fell in a battle after getting shot in the head. He came home in a casket with a flag draped over it." He was Mr. and Mrs. Horn's only child. My daddy then shared the story.

Growing up, Jimmy wasn't the greatest student in school, but he always said, "I'm gonna change the world, Daddy! Just you wait and see! I'm gonna enlist and head right off, and we'll keep the world safe!" Sure enough, as soon as he turned 18, he went and signed up. He completed boot camp and was able to come home briefly before being shipped off to war. The small town had a picnic to send him and a few others off to duty. My daddy told me the last thing Jimmy said to his daddy before he got on the bus that day was, "I'm gonna change the world, Daddy! Just you wait and see!" Mr. Horn hugged him hard and said, "You do that, son! Your mama and I will be on our knees praying 'til you get back." A tear fell from my daddy's eye as he said, "None of us could have ever known he'd never come back alive."

"But how?" I asked. Daddy went on to complete the story. Jimmy's company was called out to defuse strategic enemy strongholds one night. Upon entering and clearing the house, Jimmy and all the soldiers heard a whistling sound that began to shake the ground and house. The boys who survived said it wasn't like anything you hear in the war movies. Then came the cry, "Get down! Get down!" Jimmy hit the deck with his hands over his helmet. The missile hit the house with a force that blew the walls apart. The next thing he saw was a leg fly across the room. It was the leg of the fellow soldier Jimmy had followed into the house. All

Jimmy could hear was the ringing in his ears. He could only taste the dust that filled his lungs. He checked his own legs and arms. Everything was intact. Somehow, he had survived the blast. Instinct and training kicked in, and he picked up the now one-legged soldier, who was screaming. Those who survived recount hearing Jimmy say, "Bring them home! No soldier left behind! Let's go, soldier!"

Jimmy heroically carried his friend out the door and into the waiting vehicle. Bullets were flying all around him. They were under attack. Jimmy quickly assessed the situation. He turned to go back to pull other soldiers out. The surviving driver of the vehicle explained it this way: "He had already saved one life. He was going to get more. The moment he exited the vehicle, he dropped to the ground like a ton of bricks. I saw the blood flowing from his jaw. I knew he was dead—hit by sniper fire."

That year, Providence Street was not the street anyone wanted to be on at any time. There were several boys like Jimmy whose families lived on that street. They had all gone off to war. Many moms stayed locked inside their houses for fear the black car would be making it's dreaded run down the street to notify another set of parents they had lost their child to battle. "We had already seen it on that street twice," Daddy said. As the men stood on the front porch conveying the unthinkable, the parents dropped to their knees and all the neighbors came running or stayed on their porch, hoping the car would leave town and they weren't next.

Then came the day they went to Jimmy's house. Daddy said that the town folk recall Jimmy's mom running out into the front yard and falling face-first on the grass while weeping uncontrollably. They say Mr. Horn sat on the front porch stairs for days with the folded flag in one hand and Jimmy's helmet in the other. "I'm gonna change the world, Daddy! Just you wait and see!" He did. The war was won, and we're still free today.

When the story was over, Daddy took me across town to Jimmy's grave. Sure enough, right there on the tombstone were the words, "I'm gonna change the world, Daddy! Just you wait and see!" Daddy said Mr. Horn's wife couldn't cope and had to be admitted to the psych ward and rehab facility. Mr. Horn had to carry on with the general store. Nothing was ever the same.

Now, I knew why all the toy soldiers' faces had such angst and agony. Behind every face is a story. Some of the stories are rough. Some are pure. But for most all of them, there's somebody, somewhere who loves them or loved them. For many, there's somebody praying and hoping for their safe return home. Behind every face of those who survive, there are the scars of battle. Now, I knew why the old men tapered off their stories in tears those days as they tried to recall them to us young boys. I knew why the other men gathered around them and put hands on their shoulders.

Weeks later, once again, we were playing with toy soldiers at Mr. Horn's General Store. As always, when I packed up my soldiers and put them in the bag, Mr. Horn recounted them to make sure all the soldiers were going to make it home. Carefully scrutinizing the bag, he said, "There's only 47 here. You've left one behind. They all have to make it home!" I took Mr. Horn by the hand, and we walked through town that day. It was the day after Memorial Day, and all the flags were still waving in the warm breezes. We walked up the grassy hill that led to Jimmy's grave. As we approached, I pointed out the 48th toy soldier, standing guard at the base of Jimmy's grave. I had placed it there the day before. I turned to Mr. Horn and said, "They all made it home, sir, torn and tattered, but they all made it home because of the sacrifice of the one. And because Jimmy was a God-fearing man, I suspect he's home now, too." Mr. Horn knelt down and shed a few tears. Now, it was my hand on his shoulder.

"I'm gonna change the world, Daddy. Just you wait and see!" I never knew Jimmy personally. But he finished his mission. He changed my world and the lives of a lot of other people as well. That's why, to this day, we make the trip down to Jimmy's grave, lay a toy soldier at the base, and thank the Lord for sacrifice and freedom. We follow that with a salute to Mr. Horn and his wife, who are buried beside Jimmy. I suspect they're home with Jimmy as well.

Graduation and Leaving Home

20

How They Linger

To my knowledge, other than a class graduation photo, I have only one picture of my high school graduation, and that is to my discredit. Worse yet, I have little memory of it. In my haste and immaturity, I was oblivious to the epic nature of the moment before me. I was completely unaware of my surroundings, as well as the brevity and weight of this moment in time. To this day, it remains a point of contrition and remorse for me. You only get one high school graduation. This moment crashes into your life, lands briefly, and seems to exit as quickly as it came.

Only four short years had passed since my high school graduation. Thankfully, in those years, I grew up and matured a bit. I now stood in a long line of college graduates waiting to march victoriously onto the Academic Quad and receive diplomas.

As the marching music began, suddenly, I was overwhelmed with emotions I could not explain. Just minutes before this moment, someone had leaned over to me and said, "It's the best of times and the worst of times." Strangely, it was the first time I had ever heard this term. But at this moment, I knew exactly what it meant. Even more concretely, I felt exactly what it meant. Unlike in high school, I was aware of the moment before me. And yes, I reached out, grabbed it, and squeezed it for all it was worth.

Just one day earlier, I was in the Academic Quad with my fellow classmates for commencement rehearsal. We were walking through and practicing for the big day. Professors were explaining how everything would progress. We were then instructed to be seated. The occasion that arrived next was one I had heard about, a Wingate University tradition, but I had only thought it to be a myth until it happened before my eyes. Long-time Dean and Professor to the University, Dean Haskins, stood up, and after a few challenging words, he illustriously began to sing "Precious Memories."

As he started, we weren't sure whether to be amused or reverential. But as he sang, neither happened. All of a sudden, it was as if someone had hit the pause button on life, and we were all completely still. In a span of those 3-4 minutes, my entire college experience flashed before my eyes and heart. My future stood ready to assume its role in the handoff. It seemed as if the same was happening to every other graduate gathered in the Quad that day.

Dean Haskins sang the song without accompaniment. His Southern pronouncement of the word "linger" naturally changed it to sound more like "lingah." But aptly, it drove home the point. As he hung on every "lingah," we all hung with him.

Precious Memories, how they linger, how they ever flood my soul. Oh, how they saturated my soul and emotions that moment and through the entire day. I was grateful for what I had experienced and what was to come. But I have to admit, I did not want to leave this place or these people.

In the stillness of the midnight, precious sacred scenes unfold. I had become an adult with these people. I had experienced the highs and lows of collegiate athletics with many of them. We had lived together, played together, laughed together, traveled together, and studied together. In this time, I had forged what would be some of the most enduring and best friendships of my life. They had become more than friends; they were family now.

Precious Memories fill my soul. Dean Haskins stopped singing; the air remained still and silent for only a brief moment. Everything was about to change. Nothing would ever be the same. I was saying goodbye, but I was also leaving with something that made me better than I was when I first arrived. It really was the best and worst of times.

> I was saying goodbye, but I was also leaving with something that made me better.

Back to graduation day: the graduation music called us forward. It was time to begin the ceremony. I realized this would be my final moment with this group of people in this setting and context. I was glad for what we had accomplished and how far we had come. I was sad that it was ending and that we were all going our separate ways. I was sad to leave the university and many of my professors and mentors. But I was glad to be leaving with something that made me better.

I looked to my rear. There was my family, who had sacrificed so much to get me to this point. There were my professors who poured into me, many of whom have since retired and a few who have passed. I was surrounded by people with whom I had shared life experiences for four years. Many of whom I still share life with to this day. I heard every musical note; I felt the warmth of the sun on my face, the shade cascading across the grassy ground beneath our white chairs. I smiled, I laughed, I remembered, I shouted, I danced, and yes, I even let a few tears come forth. These epic moments do not come lightly for anyone involved. They are not intended to be ordinary. They must be felt and experienced for all that they are meant to be.

Tassels moved from right to left. The pronouncement, "You're a college graduate now!" The toss of the cap into the air. Handshakes, hugs, final words, and the stark realization that even though we express with great intent, "Let's keep in touch!" life will rush us into its frenzied cycle, and "touch" will be lost to social media. Nothing would ever be the same.

By the end of the day, the campus had mostly emptied from the day's graduation events. I was one of the few graduates remaining, packing up the last pieces from my dorm room. But this time, I would not return the next fall. My dorm room door shut behind me as I took one last walk down the hall.

Whether it's you or your child, experience graduation for all it is. When the extraordinary comes along and offers to pull you out of the ordinary, always take it up on its offer.

The car is now in drive, and I am riding through campus one final time. Most of my classmates are gone. Though we promised to stay connected, many of us will lose touch over the years.

I approached the exit to the university one final time. Yes, I stopped to look back. I took one last look, one last embrace of every moment, memory, and experience. These moments ride on the winds of time ever so briefly. But they are not intended to be ordinary. You have to grab them. Thank you, God, that I had them. Now, there were other extraordinary moments ahead of me to grab.

Whether it's you or your child, experience graduation for all it is. Do not just let it be normal. Embrace it and squeeze it for everything it holds. These feelings are meant to be felt, and these moments are meant to be experienced. We cannot rush through them. When the extraordinary comes along and offers to pull you out of the ordinary, always take it up on its offer. Graduation is one of those times.

I have returned to Wingate University many times in the years since 1993. It is still a special place to me. More than that, the people I met during my time there are special to me and forever have their names etched into the history of my life. But as many times as I go back, nothing is as it was that warm spring day of May 8, 1993. Dean Haskins has long since passed. Sadly, I'm told the song is no longer part of Wingate's graduation tradition. But for those of us who had that moment, it's really true. These memories are precious, and they still flood the soul. How they linger.

21

As You Walk

I have one picture from my high school graduation ceremony. If there are other pictures that were taken that day, my mom has boxed them away somewhere, and they are not readily seen, nor have they been seen in recent memory. This I regret.

Even worse, I have little memory of that day, the moments surrounding it, or the moments leading up to it. I think the reason I remember so little of my high school graduation ceremony is that I was simply not mature enough to be fully aware of how monumental it was at the time. I'm not sure if I was just ready to leave high school and go off to play sports in college, if I was trying to "cool" my way through it, or if I was simply oblivious to the enormous nature of the moment. This, too, I regret.

I'm sure my parents were aware of the moment. Perhaps they assumed I was aware of it. Looking back, I wish someone would have made me more aware of the weight of this chapter of my life. There are hugs and handshakes that I missed, tears I should have shed, goodbyes I never said, extraordinary moments I should have taken in, friendships I never sealed or maintained, and people I never thanked. I tore through the page of this chapter of my life with little care. I wish I had taken the time to linger and absorb the immense nature of this once-in-a-lifetime chapter before turning its page.

Now, as a parent, I am beginning to watch my own children and all their friends prepare for their high school graduations. I have made a great effort to make sure my boys do not bypass or run through this moment without effect or awareness. If I could sit down with any high school senior who is preparing to graduate, I would share the following things:

Cap & Gown — You're going to put on your cap and gown frequently during this time. Each time you do, feel the gown cascade over your

> It's not just an end; it's a new beginning.

shoulders and the grip of the cap pressing on your head and messing up your hair. It is not simply a piece of material; it's a symbol of something much greater. It's a symbol that you earned this, you made it, you have people in your life who love you and believe in you, and you are not alone. It's a symbol that you have an incredible future ahead of you, and your dreams can actually come true.

Take a deep breath, close your eyes, take a look at yourself, and believe you have what it takes. Every time you put it on, give thanks to God, and believe for your greatest potential. When you take it off for the last time, take a moment and ponder. It's not just an end; it's a new beginning. Say one final prayer with it on, and thank God for His faithfulness to you.

Cards & Gifts — If you are blessed enough to get cards and gifts, make sure you take the time to write each person a thank you card. Don't use a form letter; hand-write it. Your hands will likely get tired. If they do, receive the weariness as a reminder that you are surrounded by people who care about you. For every single "i" that you dot and "t" that you cross, for every sealed envelope that you send, for every hand cramp, be reminded that someone cared enough to recognize you and pour into you. Pour yourself into every word you say and make it personal. Feel the card in your hand before you send it, and remind yourself that you are part of something bigger than yourself: a community of people who care about you.

Ceremonies & Parties — If you are blessed enough to have a church or family recognize you publicly through a ceremony, service, or party, make sure you look every single person in attendance in the eye and thank them. You may not like all the attention, but for one single moment, let yourself be overwhelmed by the fact that you mean something to other people. Take a look around the room and realize that it's not just a ritual; it's about people taking the time to let you know you matter. Take that in—all of it—and be thankful. There are many lonely people who would give their right arm to have a moment like you have right now, to be able to draw a crowd and be the center of attention in the room.

> Make sure you look every single person in attendance in the eye and thank them.

Your School Building — Take one last moment to go to your school building. Walk the halls, smell the smells, drive through the parking lot, park in your old spot, step onto your old field or court, and breathe it all in. Let the walls, hardwoods, stands, and chairs talk to you one more time. It's been said that walls cannot talk, but that's only because no one takes the time to listen. Make sure you listen one more time before you leave. Part of your story is forged here. It's forever etched in the layers of these walls, this court, or this field. Walk, be quiet, listen, and give thanks.

Let this place talk to you one more time. Every time you go back after this, it won't be the same. You won't own it the way you do right now. There may be a trophy or plaque with your name on it, but it will never be the same as it is right now. They may even remodel a room, add on, or even tear the whole place down. Take the time to listen one last time and remember. Your name is etched here forever, and while it may be forgotten by others, let it never be forgotten by you.

Teachers, Professors, Coaches, & School Officials — More important than the walls are the relationships. Take the time to personally thank the teachers who taught you, the coaches who coached you, and the people who poured into you and gave a piece of their lives to you. I assure you, few of them are doing it for the pay. They do it for you and your future. Make sure you take the time to tell them it mattered. Many of them labor in what they do, and year by year, they wonder if they can keep doing it. They are tired and weary. Your thankfulness is worth more to them than any paycheck they'll ever receive. They will be better for it and so will you.

> It's been said that walls cannot talk, but that's only because no one takes the time to listen.

Here's an even greater challenge. If there is a particular teacher or coach you didn't like or you feel didn't do the best job, work up the courage to go and thank them also. It will build your humility and prepare you for a lifetime of dealing with people who won't be your favorites but who still need your love. Life is full of them. It's also highly likely that even though they may not show it at the time, your effort is what will tear out one brick of their hard exterior that's been built up through a life of wounds you know nothing about. You will be better for it, and so will they.

Your Parents & Family — Take the time to thank your parents, siblings, and all other family members who invested in you. Even if your parents were dysfunctional and crummy, take the time to thank them. As you did in thanking any teachers who were a bit dysfunctional, do so even more with your parents and family members.

Your parents are not only grieving the loss of your childhood but also the fact that you are moving into a new chapter of life. You're not the little kid who used to crawl into bed beside them or run into their arms anymore. The old toys that brought such joy on Christmas Day are soon to be packed up. The memories will be boxed up, and while they will never stop being your parents, they will feel as if they're more a part of your past than your future. Remember how much they love you and gave up for you. They are much of the reason for the person you are today. They invested in you and gave everything for you, and they likely always will. Don't forsake or forget them. Always call them, thank them, go back to check on them, tell them you love them, and give them the biggest hug possible. Keep them in your life. Never forget the road that leads back home.

> Never forget the road that leads back home.

Though you may not think it now, you will always need them more than you know. Don't wake up one day and say to yourself, "I wish I could hear their voices one more time." If you have them today, keep them and make the most of it.

In addition, if your parents worked too much, were absentee parents, or took little time for you, be intentional to forgive them, even if they don't deserve it. It's the only way you'll ever be free of the wounds that caused them to do those things to you, even if they didn't mean to do so.

Friendships — If you have broken relationships, mend them—now. It doesn't matter how great the hurt may be. Years from now, the trivial things you may be holding a grudge for will not be worth it. Let go of the wound now. There will be plenty else in life that will try to wound you. Learn to deal with those things now so that those unforgiven wounds don't become the dysfunction that cripples you in life.

Purpose in your mind to keep the friendships you have forged in this part of your life. Sadly, most of these friendships will fade with time. The people you shared such close moments with will likely one day become mere acquaintances or even strangers. But there will be a few that may last into adulthood, even a lifetime. If those friendships mean anything to you, purpose to keep them. To have a friend, you'll have to *be* a friend. You may have to make the first contact, even when you feel like no one ever contacts you. That's okay, do it anyway. Some of those friendships are worth the investment. I wish I had done the same.

> Years from now, the trivial things you may be holding a grudge for will not be worth it. Let go of the wound now.

Scripture — When my first-born son, Jadon, graduated from high school in 2022, it was only a year later when he had all four of his wisdom teeth removed. Immediately following the surgery, he came into the house, went straight to the bathroom, and began to vomit blood into a bucket I was holding in front of his mouth while his arms were draped over my shoulder. He was in intense pain and still suffering from the after-effects of the anesthesia. At this moment, with tears flowing down his cheeks, he began to say out loud, "So do not fear, for I am with you; do not be dismayed, for I am your God. I will strengthen you and help you; I will uphold you with my righteous right hand" (Isaiah 41:10, NIV). I began to cry as he quoted it.

This was the first Bible verse I ever committed to memory when I was about Jadon's age. I did so because my aunt called me and shared this verse with me over the phone the night before I had reconstructive knee surgery in high school. I immediately memorized the verse and quoted it to myself as they put me to sleep before my own surgery the next morning. As a result, when my boys were little, I would sit on their beds every night before bedtime and quote the verse with them out loud before their bedtime prayers. Until this moment of trauma with Jadon after his surgery, I never knew the verse took. But there he was, quoting it many years later, through his tears and pain, "So do not fear, for I am with you; do not be dismayed, for I am your God. I will strengthen you and help you; I will uphold you with my righteous right hand." He never forgot.

God's Word and His promises will sustain you in the most joyous times and in the lowest moments of your life.

You must center your life on the Word of God and your faith. Nothing else will be as important. You must read His Word each and every day and commit as much of it to memory as you can. As the Bible states in James 1:22 (NLT), "But don't just listen to God's word. You must do what it says...". God's Word and His promises will sustain you in the most joyous times and in the lowest moments of your life. At times, His Words will be the only thing you have to hold on to that makes any sense.

But hear me, in order for it to be alive to you in life's most traumatic moments (as it was with Jadon), it must come alive to you in life's most mundane moments (as it did with my boys each night before bed). Hold to it, and you will never break apart, no matter what life may throw at you.

Graduation Day — When the day to march finally arrives, be sure to take in every moment. Let yourself feel every ounce of laughter, joy, anticipation, excitement, nervousness, and yes, if there are tears, let them flow. It's not a sign of weakness or sadness. It's a moment worthy of every emotion. Let yourself experience all of them. When "Pomp & Circumstance" begins to play, and you begin to march, be sure you take in every step. Look in front of you, look behind you, look at the room. This is a moment where life is lifted above the ordinary. This is a moment where the natural collides with the supernatural. This moment—this one, single, solitary moment of your life—is where the ordinary and the extraordinary intersect, and you are right in the middle of it. Make sure you notice it. It only comes once in a lifetime with this group of people. It will never happen again. Don't run through it.

This is the last time you will ever be together like this with these people—the ones you grew up with, rode the bus with, played with, cried with, laughed with, and shared life with. Sure, you may see some of them again, but some you will never see again. But whether you see them again or not, it will never be like this again. Make sure you look around. Don't just look to the front; look behind, beside, and all around so you see it all. This group will never gather in this way again. Look up in the stands and give your parents a smile, make eye contact, and share a tear. It is one moment in time, and you are at its center. Take every picture, give every hug, give every last goodbye, shed every tear, and hold every moment you can before you leave. You will only have it once. Squeeze everything out of it that you can. Take it from a guy who didn't and wished he had.

Most Importantly — Somewhere in the middle of all this *epic,* you must take a moment to go to your knees and thank the God who makes all this possible. Regardless of your thoughts toward Him, what you may or may not know about Him, or what you think you know of Him, He has made you "fearfully and wonderfully" (Psalm 139:14). This

> Take every picture, give every hug, give every last goodbye, shed every tear, and hold every moment you can before you leave.

moment in which you are currently standing is one of the most fearful and wonderful moments you will ever have. It was designed for you. You are not here by accident. The world is before you, heaven is shining on you, and God is inviting you forward to achieve your potential. Every moment in your life has been connected to this one significant achievement. Your first steps as a toddler, your first day of school, your last day of elementary school, your first day of high school, the sporting events, the school plays, the

You must take a moment to go to your knees and thank the God who makes all this possible.

assemblies, the family gatherings, the vacations, the wins, the losses, the tears, the joys, the birthday parties—every moment has led you to this one moment, and they are all connected. That is roughly 6,500 days of God's faithfulness and guidance in your life. Take the time to thank Him, be humble, and as you do, hold out your hand and let Him lead you into the next chapter. It only gets better.

22

Where The Geese Fly

The day had finally arrived. I knew it was coming. I had tried to prepare myself for it, but it still hit me like a sledgehammer. This was the day we would take my firstborn son, Jadon, off to college. I had spent the last ten months of his high school senior year trying to ready myself for the emotions of this day, but nothing could prepare me for what I felt and experienced.

It began the first day of high school, almost a year earlier. The moment Jadon and my middle son, Ryder, a high school freshman at the time, drove off to school together at 6:45 a.m. with the morning sun rising over their heads, I stood alone in the driveway and cried as I watched them drive away. It seemed only seconds ago that they were little kids, and we were all racing bikes in the driveway and shooting each other with Nerf guns. Now, they were grown teenagers. Though many had warned me, I was still stunned by how fast time had flown.

Little did I know, the tears I shed that morning would only be the first of many over the next several months. I prayed with them and watched them drive away every day of that year. I tried to soak up every moment. I knew time was fleeting. Though I tried to stop or slow it down, it seemed to sift through my hands like sand in an hourglass.

By 9:00 a.m. that departing day for college, two cars were packed fully with clothes, more shoes than I care to count, a microwave, a mini refrigerator, and a handful of mementos to help Jadon feel at home, though he was going to be geographically far away.

It had all been planned. The last thing Jadon would do before pulling out of the driveway was pull up the sign in the front yard that had been announcing to the world for the last three months that he was an official high school graduate. It would be the last turn, the last official act that would move him from high school to college, from youth to adult. That part alone would be difficult.

> Though many had warned me, I was still stunned by how fast time had flown.

Sure, on the surface it was just a sign, but beneath the surface, it was so much more. It was the turning of a page from his childhood, the first eighteen years of his life, into adulthood. Personally, I had to grieve the loss of his childhood, and so did he. It was not easy, but it was necessary. The tears were not so much because of what we were leaving behind, but more tears of gratitude that we even got to do it. Every moment of his childhood had been a dream, and we were thankful for it. This was why taking down the sign was more than just taking down a sign. Jadon knew it, I knew it, his mom knew it, and even his younger brothers knew it.

I think this is a necessary life transition many people bypass too easily. If you have children, there comes a time when you put up the toys, the balls, and all that goes with it for the last time. Some things you may keep for a lifetime, but to most, you will have to say "Goodbye" and "Thank you." I had to let myself grieve the passing of that childhood for

Jadon, and so did he. Sure, it was an exciting time ahead, and life was far from over, but this chapter was over.

As a pastor, I've sat in counseling sessions with far too many people who were never aware of this process. Others were perhaps so acutely aware of the process that they tried to suppress or ignore it because they didn't want to labor through the associated emotion or trauma. When that trauma is not dealt with properly, it comes out later as unidentifiable wounds. At that point, we try to deal with those wounds in unhealthy ways. Many couples wake up years later, look at each other, and realize they don't know how to live with each other apart from their kids. Sadly, they decide to end their marriage covenant and split their family. I knew I could not let that happen. So, I allowed myself to cry and process all of the emotions that came, and I didn't apologize. I knew I would be better and healthier for it down the road. Taking down the graduation yard sign that day would not just be taking down any old sign. We all knew it, but it had to happen.

> Some things you may keep for a lifetime, but to most, you will have to say "Goodbye" and "Thank you."

The moment that came right before we took down the sign was a moment I had not planned and I was completely unprepared. We all stood in the driveway. My wife was standing by her car, ready to drive off. My other two boys were in the garage. Jadon stood beside me. These were the last moments. One of the primary reasons Jadon was leaving that day was because he was getting to live out his dream of playing college basketball. It was a dream we had worked on and trained for in that very driveway for most of his life up until this point.

Spontaneously, I grabbed a basketball, bounce-passed it to Jadon, and said, "Okay, one last shot before you go off to become a college basketball player!" Jadon received the ball, turned to his right, and dribbled around the sidewalk behind the house. Unknown to me, emotions were beginning to overwhelm him, and he didn't want us to see. As he turned back toward the goal, he broke, let out a sigh and a loud "Gosh!" and began to weep on the spot, ball in hand.

Everything fell. His mom stood motionless at the car, not knowing how to deal with the moment. His two brothers moved up the driveway and toward the yard in the opposite direction. They didn't want anyone to see the tears running down their faces, so they tried to avoid the scene. I began to weep. I ran toward Jadon, grabbed and hugged him, and said, "It's okay. Let it out—all of it. It's okay." In a moment frozen in time, we stood there weeping in each other's arms. Thankfully, my middle son Ryder was astute enough to catch that moment on camera. Though I'm thankful for it, the picture doesn't do the moment justice.

> I allowed myself to cry and process all of the emotions that came, and I didn't apologize.

Not caught on camera is what happened next. Right when Jadon and I were weeping and hugging, a flock of geese flew over us in a perfectly formed "V." They were honking and chirping to the top of their lungs. I stopped, looked up at them, and held my arm on Jadon's shoulder. Jadon stepped forward, swished his last shot in the driveway, and then turned to go get the sign. Through tears, gasps for air, and solemnity, he walked the sign back up the driveway to the garage. It was done. It was epic. Time to turn the page.

For days leading up to and following this moment, multiple people sent me texts and pictures with a similar theme, "You've done your job. It's time to let them leave the nest. Give them wings and let them fly. Let them fly like eagles." I was truly thankful for these notes and their encouragement. I knew they loved me and meant well. It all even looked good on a postcard or GIF and sounded right. After all, eagles are far more majestic than geese—right!? But I took a different posture on the matter.

I never viewed parenting Jadon or any of my boys as a job or even a responsibility. Don't get me wrong, I know that it is a great responsibility with considerable accountability. But for my wife and me, our posture was never, "It's our job to raise you for 18 years, and then you're on your own!" We took it day by day, and we showed up to love each other and our children in the good, bad, beautiful, ugly, easy, and hard. We have always been their parents, and as far as we're concerned, though our roles will change and decrease over the years, we will always be their parents. None of it has ever been task-driven; we are motivated by an intense love for our boys and an overwhelming sense of gratitude to God.

But what of the geese flying in a "V" motion, who seemed to interrupt our epic moment? Far from interruption, I believe they were sent on a mission to remind me of an important truth.

When geese fly, they fly in a "V" shape for specific reasons. One reason is that it conserves energy because this formation reduces wind resistance. In this formation, birds can fly great distances without stopping or getting tired. Pelicans or eagles who fly alone beat their wings more frequently and have higher heart rates than birds who fly in formation. Fighter pilots fly in formation for many of the same reasons.

The geese take turns in front and change positions frequently. Some lead and then fall back for others to lead, then they go back up and lead again. All the while, the other birds honk to encourage each other to keep going and not give up. They also honk to keep track of each other and know that everyone is together, which leads to the other reason for the "V" formation.

In this formation, the geese can more easily keep track of each other and make sure no one is lost or left behind.

They are constantly communicating, never leaving each other, always encouraging each other, and constantly changing lead positions but always moving together. This is something I have always known because I have used this illustration for sermons concerning how church members should do life together. But the moment that flock of geese flew over us, I discovered a truth, even though it didn't sound as majestic: this isn't eagles leaving nests; this is geese changing positions.

Jadon will always be my son. He will always have a home with me. At his current age and the time of this writing, the frontal lobe of his brain isn't even fully developed yet. He still needs me to be a parent. I will never stop being his dad. Sure, responsibilities and accountabilities change, grow, and deepen, but I will always be his dad. He's not flying away on his own; we're just starting to change positions in the flock. Now, he is getting to experience what it's like to be out front, and I am learning what it's like to move to the back and cheer. There will still be times when I need to move back out in front, and now, there will be more times when I need to move to the back. But together, we still fly.

Lord willing, there will come a time when we add to the flock. There will be geese from other flocks who will join ours, and vice versa. Lord willing, there will even be little goslings who join the flock, but together, we all still fly. I will move further and further to the rear of the flock, but I will be ready for that when it comes, and I will still continue to cheer and honk with the best of them. But together, we all still fly. There are no empty nests and no flying in isolation. We are one flock, relying on each other—always have been, always will be, and that will not change.

One day, my time will come to leave the earthly flock, and I'll get a new set of wings. Old signs will come down, and new signs will be put up. Tears will be shed, and epic moments shared. Memories will hold us together until we are united again in the heavenly flock, where we will fly higher than we have ever flown before. There, we will talk about the day when geese flew over our house and reminded us that no one flies in isolation and that we are one flock. We'll thank God that every moment before, in between, and after that day was knit together in His perfect plan of formation.

Trauma, Weakness, and The Valley

23

This Is Trauma

This is trauma. The week began like any other week. That is when trauma decided to make its uninvited way into the serenity of my life—Tuesday at 4:35 p.m. My youngest son, Baylon, called, "Dad, Nana has fallen, and mom is calling 911! You gotta come home now!" As soon as I hung up and began to make my way to the car, I knew the events of my life for this week would drastically change. Trauma has a way of doing that.

As I arrived home, the ambulance was about to carry my mom to the emergency room at the local hospital. My youngest son Baylon had come in from school and found her lying on the floor of our home in a pool of blood, contorted and broken from her fall. She had come to give him a piano lesson. That trauma will likely leave its mark on him for the rest of his life.

My wife called 911. I cleaned up the blood and then made my way to the ER. The diagnosis included one fractured pelvis, a potentially

> God will not waste our trauma. When we entrust ourselves to God, trauma and pain don't subtract from our story; they add to it.

fractured hip, and a shattered shoulder, with an emergency shoulder replacement imminent. An inch or two to the left or right, and the fall could have left her dead. Thankfully, the blood was from her arm and not her head.

In the meantime, my wife's father had disappeared, and no one could find him. When they finally checked on him, they found him on his knees at his bedside. No one could determine how long he had been there. He'd had a possible stroke or heart attack and had a definite urinary tract infection and confusion. He remained isolated to the ER with no visitors, as the hospital in Roanoke, VA, was on lockdown due to a COVID outbreak.

This is trauma. Uninvited, unwelcome, disturbing, painful, unnerving, always jarring, and never harmonious with the rhythms of your desired pattern of life. There will always be harder stories of trauma than ours, and there will always be easier stories of trauma than ours. No one needs to apologize for the severity or lack of severity of their own trauma. Trauma is part of our stories, which are given to us for a reason. Sure, God may not have intended for us to face certain parts of our trauma. Yes, some of our trauma is self-induced. But much of it is not. Either way, God will not waste our trauma. It will inevitably become part of our story, which will make us better, as unpleasant as it may seem when we're going through it.

> In this world you will have trouble. But take heart! I have overcome the world.
>
> JOHN 16:33B

I know this because of verses and promises in the Bible like John 16:33b (NIV): "In this world you will have trouble. But take heart! I have overcome the world." Notice that Jesus said, "will have trouble," not "might have trouble." Yes, the reality is that I will experience trauma and difficulty.

Some may not be pleasant. But in the midst of that, I will be reminded that I hold in my possession what is always God's best, even when I don't understand it. The world can never take that from me or overcome it.

Passages like James 1:2-4 (NLT) also reassure me. "When troubles of any kind come your way, consider it an opportunity for great joy. For you know that when your faith is tested, your endurance has a chance to grow. So let it grow, for when your endurance is fully developed, you will be perfect and complete, not lacking anything."

> When troubles of any kind come your way, consider it an opportunity for great joy. For you know that when your faith is tested, your endurance has a chance to grow. So let it grow, for when your endurance is fully developed, you will be perfect and complete, not lacking anything.
>
> JAMES 1:2-4

This means trauma reintroduces me to a better definition of joy—one deeper than I could imagine myself. It introduces me to a joy that is not built on external circumstances. It helps me see that before I can truly define loss and pain, I must first be able to define goodness and true joy—and where and Who that joy comes from.

The reality is I cannot define true joy by way of comfort or a life void of pain. This helps me see that the circumstances of my life can be perfect and fulfilling in my own eyes, yet my story could still be incomplete in the eyes of the One Who is writing it, and Who has written it from beginning to end. It reminds me that I don't get to control the outcomes; my responsibility is to trust, even when it makes no sense. This is the faith I have built my life upon. What other options do I have? As Simon Peter said in John 6:68

(ESV), "Lord, to whom shall we go? You have the words of eternal life." I've tried some of the others. They never satisfy long-term.

The world is not safe. It never will be fully safe. It is filled with trauma. For followers of Jesus, this world is not our ultimate home. It was never meant to be our ultimate home. Strangely, we live in a world desperately trying to insulate itself from the possibility of harm and trauma. I'm certainly not saying we go looking for trauma, or that we don't use the common sense God gave us or exercise personal responsibility. But I am suggesting that if we seek so desperately to insulate ourselves from every trouble, we will deprive ourselves of the beautiful redemption our fractures can display. That beauty is what allows us to cast aside our worries and fears.

> For followers of Jesus, this world is not our ultimate home.
>
> In fear of trauma and death, we invite many other less notable deaths into our lives.

The only downside to the advancements of modern science and medicine is that they have a way of elevating the idea that somehow medicine is going to solve the problem of trauma, suffering, and death, as if they can be fixed. No amount of medical advancement will ever solve our problems because they are part of the natural course of life and eternity. They are not to be fixed. Like it or not, they give life its substance and meaning. As Scripture says in Ecclesiastes 3:1, "To everything, there is a season."

Sure, no one wants to die before their time, and thankfully, God has taken pleasure in using modern medicine to have its place in the cycle of life and our stories. But in fear of trauma and death, we invite many other less notable deaths into our lives: death of dreams, marriages and families, hopes, abilities, spirituality and faith, community and relationship, commitment and fight, and the promise of something greater. Strangely, trying to avoid trauma and death inevitably causes us to live life less abundantly. That death is far greater than the ultimate death we're trying to avoid. For the believer, death leads to ultimate life in glory. This world is not our ultimate home.

The truth is that when we entrust ourselves to God, trauma and pain don't subtract from our story; they add to it. Jesus said in John 10:10 (NKJV), "I have come that they may have life, and that they may have it more abundantly."

> I have come that they may have life, and that they may have it more abundantly.
>
> JOHN 10:10

Don't forget that this is the same guy who had the greatest post-traumatic story ever. Jesus went from death to resurrection and from there to eternal glory. Trauma was not the end of His story; it was only the beginning. All who put their trust in Him are part of the same story.

I spent hours in the ER and at the hospital by my mom's side the week after her fall. Hours on the road back and forth and hours waiting and praying. I could have focused on the 96 hours of trauma poured into my story that week by the brokenness of the world in which we live. I could have let that drive me to a worldly response, tear me down, or cause me to do something that would give me temporary satisfaction.

The other choice is that I could let the trauma remind me that, in spite of this broken world in which we live, I'd spent most of my years with my mom in blessing after blessing. That reminded me once again that even though trauma had surrounded me, the loudest voice was, is, and always has been the truth that I've gotten way more blessings than I ever deserved. This is trauma, and this is how God uses it: pointing us to what is best and good.

24

Something

I put the last of my mom's personal belongings into the white plastic bag the hospital had given me. A few sticks of gum, one package of cough drops, a cell phone, a pair of shoes, and one pair of clothes—that was it. Outside, the ambulance waited to transport her to the next location of her long road to what we hoped and prayed would be recovery. The pain medication likely made her unaware of my presence, but I hugged her goodbye anyway.

I walked downstairs to my car with the white bags sagging my shoulders and weighing down each of my hands, praying and hoping I would not be back for a while. Visiting hours had long ended, and the night was serene and very cold. As I sat in my car and placed the bags on the passenger's side, I noticed that her clothes were still stained from the blood that saturated them the day she fell. I came to the realization that this bag was all that marked the last 15 days of her grueling stay in the hospital. All she had talked about in those 15 days was leaving the hospital, and now we were finally leaving.

But she wasn't much better, and she wasn't going home. She was going to the next place and the next chapter. The road ahead still seemed long and arduous. I breathed in the crisp, cold air, closed my eyes, and exhaled for probably the first time in two weeks. I held the moment close to my chest for a minute. At least I was exhaling for a change and not hyperventilating. At least it was a step. It wasn't much, but it was something.

As I began to thank the Lord for the "something" in that moment, I began to realize how much my life overflows with "something." Though stress, trauma, and crisis had characterized the last two weeks of my life, it was still completely swallowed up by "something."

Every night after I left the hospital, I came home to a wife and three boys. That was something. I had a warm bed and a soft mattress. That was something. I had water that flowed out of a faucet on demand. I could even change the temperature of the water with the turn of a nozzle. That was something. Clothes on my back, shoes on my feet, a temperature-controlled house, those were something. A pantry full of food, mostly due to church members who loved and supported me, boy, that was something. I could grab a fork, bend my elbow, and bring food to my mouth with the most precise level of coordination. That was something. I know because it was something I had to do for my mom the first few days of her stay in the hospital because she couldn't feed herself. Sadly, you don't realize how littered your life is with the blessing of "something" until the trauma of life threatens to take it away or disrupt it.

> It wasn't much, but it was something. Sadly, you don't realize how littered your life is with the blessing of "something" until the trauma of life threatens to take it away or disrupt it.

The "somethings" of life are those commonplace activities and rhythms that take place in the mundane moments of what we assume to be conventional life. They are generally wedged in between the trauma and crisis we try to avoid and the next big, pleasurable moment we hope for. We rarely notice our "somethings" because we take them for granted and form the notion that they are somehow owed to us. Yet, they are the very things that are meant to give life its fullness; they are gifts from God given specifically to us on a daily basis.

The Scriptures tell us in Ecclesiastes 3:12-13 (NIV), "I know there is nothing better for people than to be happy and to do good while they live. That each of them may eat and drink, and find satisfaction in all their toil—this is the gift of God." Eating, drinking, everyday living, working, toil, and all the things that happen in the remarkable routine of life—the things we generally take for granted—are all "gifts of God." They all find their gathering in the folder of "something," and they are quite miraculous.

> I know there is nothing better for people than to be happy and to do good while they live. That each of them may eat and drink, and find satisfaction in all their toil— this is the gift of God.
>
> ECCLESIASTES 3:12-13

Are you aware of how many optic nerves have to align so you can see to make that left turn on the way to work? Gift. That is something. Are you aware of how the brain filters out all the irrelevant sounds around you so that you can hear that song or that person's voice? Gift. Miracle. That is something. It would be enough for us to put food in our mouths and swallow it to survive. But God gave us taste buds so that we could enjoy the process. Amazing gift. That's something.

Because my mother had trouble getting food from the plate to her mouth, there were many meals during my mom's hospital stay when I ate by myself and marveled at the miracle of simply being able to bend my elbow, bring food to my mouth, have the teeth to chew it up, the saliva glands to push it down my throat, and the stomach to process it. But most of all, the taste buds to taste it and the pleasure that brought to me. Gift. That's something.

You feel the emotions that produce tears. That's something. At least you can feel. When your cheeks hurt from smiling and laughing too hard, that's something. The difficulty of making a choice on the menu and realizing you not only have money in your pocket to pay for food but choices in what you eat. That's something. When you realize your pain, loss, and suffering are the beginning of your insight and offer the opportunity to be better, that's something. When you face a personal crisis and are surrounded by people who love and support you, making you realize life moves at the pace of relationship and not technology, that's something.

> I know that everything God does will endure forever; nothing can be added to it and nothing taken from it. God does it so that people will fear him.
>
> ECCLESIASTES 3:14

But the best part about "something" is found in Ecclesiastes 3:14 (NIV): "I know that everything God does will endure forever; nothing can be added to it and nothing taken from it. God does it so that people will fear him." So, if the routine "somethings" of my life (everyday living, eating, drinking, toil, and work) are all a "gift of God" and all of these will "endure forever," that means every single "something" of my life is eternal and has meaning and purpose. Every "something" of my life is not just for here but also for eternity. Every "something" is doing something, and none of it is random, no matter how routine it may seem.

> Every "something" of my life is not just for here but also for eternity.

When the waters rise and life closes in, remember your "somethings." Your life is littered with them, and they have a purpose. They are not routine, random, or commonplace. They are meant to remind you of how full life can be, even when it's hard. But they are also meant to remind you that this earthly life is temporary and leads to something beyond description: the glory to come. That's something. Actually, that's everything.

25

The Power of Weakness

From the bedroom of the house we were renting in Florida, I heard the crash of chairs and the wall buckle from across the house. I darted out, only to find my mom on the floor, cane at her side, the victim of another fall. I picked her up, dusted her off, pressed her to my chest, and told her it was going to be alright. This scene played out more than once for me that summer.

There is a moment in life when your parents grow weak and you have to come running to pick them up. Yes, the ones you used to call to come running and pick you up are now calling you to come running. This transition to parenting your parents is one of life's most difficult ones. My parents, once so robust and strong, have grown older. Simple tasks are no longer simple. Everything is hard now. Watching them grow weak has not been easy.

> This transition to parenting your parents is one of life's most difficult ones.

As I was picking my mom up off the ground and holding her, my mind darted back to those days when she used to come running to pick me up off the ground and hold me. She always came running—always. The image of a parent running to pick up their child after they have fallen seems so wonderfully transcendent and right. These moments, though generally brought on by trauma we'd prefer to avoid, are some of life's divine gifts. The moments when your child's tears soak into your shirt and run down your neck after you tell them everything will be alright are some of life's most fitting and valued moments. But those moments are born in weakness. When a parent's strength collides with their child's weakness, something divine takes place.

Sadly, in our fast-paced culture, the image of a child running to pick up their parent seems callous and unnatural. It can be tiresome and make even the strongest weary. It challenges every fiber of the relationship and pushes a level of trauma into our lives that we would prefer to avoid. Yet, strangely, these moments, too, have this incredible ability to lift us above the ordinary and make the miraculous out of the mundane.

> My grace is sufficient for you, for My power is made perfect in weakness.
>
> 2 CORINTHIANS 12:9

But if you allow the weight of the burden to crush you, if you wish yourself to be somewhere else when life gets most difficult, you will miss the strength born out of weakness.

The Lord says in 2 Corinthians 12:9 (ESV), "My grace is sufficient for you, for My power is made perfect in weakness." It is generally at the corner of life's most difficult moments that you meet the miraculous. When mixed with faith, it is at the corner of your weakness that you encounter the divine. It's by design.

Wonder is not always found in the most desirable tasks. Sometimes, it's on the other side of some of the most challenging and undesirable tasks. It's not difficult to show up for the spectacular and pleasurable moments of life. But showing up for the tedious, mundane, and difficult tasks can lead us to what we need most in this life: God's power.

Sometimes, you have to show up for the life you didn't sign up for. You'll have to show up by the hospital bed, the graveside, the cancer treatment, the marriage that seems to be breaking apart, the disappointment, the hurt, the tiresome job, the ailing body, the screaming child, and yes, the aging parent. You won't think you have the strength to do it, and the reality is you don't. But that's the point. Here, you learn to rely on God's strength and not your own. Here you find that the gift of your weakness can actually lead you to His perfect strength.

> Sometimes, you have to show up for the life you didn't sign up for.

That's why you show up: because there, in the midst of the painful parts of life, something is waiting for us all. It is something we get nowhere else, a supernatural strength that enables us to press on and prepares us for glory in heaven. We find God's power here, lifting us above the ordinary. Here in our brokenness, we find the fullness of His mercy and strength and discover nothing else as satisfying, even when our brokenness and weakness usher it in.

26
The Valley

The day was cool, crisp, and beautiful. The colors of fall had reached their resplendent fullness. The brightly-colored leaves were putting on their dazzling display in the mountains of Southern Virginia. My wife, our three boys, and I had gathered at the foot of the mountain that was considered to be the highest peak in this area. We tightened our shoelaces, zipped up our hoodies, and covered our heads. The hike to the summit of the mountain would be long. We had a full day ahead. Though our body temperatures would rise with physical exertion, the air temperature around us would drop throughout the ascent. We were excited and ready for a full day of vigor.

We came to the trailhead and began our climb. The higher we went, the steeper the trail. Along the way to the summit, there were several moments to stop and catch exquisite views of the countryside we left behind. There were moments to pull off, take a breath, get refreshment, enjoy the journey, enjoy each other's company, and remind ourselves how much fun we were having. But these were also reminders of the physical nature of the trip. They were reminders that we needed to pace ourselves and encourage each other to push forward. There was still much work to be done. We needed to stay together to get to the top.

As we approached the top of the mountain, the ground beneath us became more jagged and rough. The rocks and roots beneath us became more like steps. Our breathing became more labored. The air became colder and the wind more cutting. But each element of nature only served to exhilarate and stimulate us as we pushed onward and upward. We were close. The goal was within our grasp. We could see it just ahead.

Finally, we arrived. The top of the mountain was as majestic as advertised. The views of the mountains surrounding us and the valleys below were unmatched. The panorama of beauty took our breath away with each glimpse. We climbed from rock to rock, over and under, back and forth, to take in every aspect of the beauty. We smiled, snapped pictures, lingered, and took in the wonder of it all.

> Very little grows on top of the mountain. The valley is what makes the mountaintop view so beautiful.

There were lakes below and flowery, lush green, and even brown meadows. Birds were gliding through the air all around us. The sky was a perfect blue. The sun provided enough warmth to make the moment pleasing, despite the air's chill.

It was in the stillness of this majesty, looking around, that I noticed something I never had before in all of my mountaintop experiences. On top of the mountain, we were surrounded mostly by rocks, dirt, and the occasional grassy sprout. The flowery meadows, colorful leaves, and marvelous lakes were all beneath us in the valley we left behind. The rocks, dirt, and grassy sprouts on the mountaintop contained a beauty of their own, but they paled in comparison to the beauty in the valley below. Very little grows on top of the mountain.

We didn't make this physical, tiring ascent to see the baldness of the mountaintop. We made the ascent to look back at the valley. From the top, we had a different perspective. Most of the beauty was in the valley below. In fact, it was the valley that made the view from the mountaintop so beautiful. There would be little to look upon without the wonder of the valley.

> There is value in the valley that can only be attained in the valley.

Few live on the mountaintop; most live in the valley. I suppose you can live on top of the mountain, and some people make their lives there. But to get what you need, you'll always have to go down into the valley for sustenance. Perhaps God designed life this way.

The mountaintop provides us with an exuberant experience, but only for a moment. We aren't designed to stay there permanently. Little growth takes place on top of the mountain. It's refreshing to go there, but for most of us, the living, breathing, working, and dying are all done in the valley. The valley is where most of the growing takes place. The valley is what makes the mountaintop view so beautiful because it contains a beauty of its own. The mountaintop serves to give us the proper perspective of the valley.

Many spend their entire lives trying to live off of or get to the mountaintop experience. We attempt to ascend from one summit to another. There is excitement in that journey, and some of it has purpose. The ascent serves to give us clear and defined goals. It can refresh and invigorate us. It can motivate us and give us needed discipline. The view at the end of the ascent is rewarding. But we aren't meant to stay on the mountaintop. Growth occurs in the valley. There is value in the valley that can only be attained in the valley.

Along each summit journey in life, as we cross over the adversities and challenges of each season, there will be moments to stop, reflect on what we left behind, and consider what is most important. There will be moments to remind us of the joy in the journey. There will be moments to remind us how fortunate we are to enjoy the company of those we love and journey with to the summit. There will be moments to encourage and push each other forward through each challenge, difficulty, and disappointment. There will be the moment when we reach the top and celebrate the defining accomplishment of a goal. The view from the top will give us the proper perspective of things below. That is the moment we will be reminded of what is most important. There is incredible wonder in the valley.

Never fail to be in awe of the beautiful routine.

Beauty, growth, and sustenance are all in the valley. The valley is where the working and living are done from day to day. The valley is where most of us will be called to live. At first glance, it won't seem to hold the excitement of the mountaintop. It may seem mundane and routine. But look again. Remember what you saw when you were on the mountain peak. The valley is far from routine. The valley has incredible significance for life. The valley is where most everything grows. The beautiful, the awful, the good, the hard—most of it takes place in the day-to-day of the valley.

The valley is anything but boring. It is anything but mundane. With proper perspective, the valley can be exciting. The day-to-day of the valley has incredible potential and majesty. It may take an occasional ascent to the mountaintop to see it, but remember, there is no incredible, majestic, mountaintop view without the awe and reverence of the valley.

When you come down from the top of the mountain, you'll need to remind yourself of this fact because you will

spend most of your life in the day to day of the valley, trudging back and forth from one routine task to another. But
never fail to be in awe of the beautiful routine. This is your
life, and this is where most of the growth God has designed
for you will take place, right in the middle of your own flowery meadow in the valley.

Your valley is filled with lush meadows. It may consist
of sunsets and sunrises daily. It may consist of the drive to
work and the drive home. It may consist of crying children
and bedtime prayers. It may consist of the labor of preparing dinner for the family. It may consist of a tiring day at
work. It may consist of practices and rehearsals, programs,
walking the dog, or simply taking out the trash—again and
again and again. But make no mistake, in the middle of that
valley, your valley, you are surrounded by a majesty meant
to grow you and make you better.

Your valley will also be filled with trauma, adversity, disappointment, and trying times. You aren't meant to escape
those things. Some of them will come by God's design. Some
will come simply due to the broken world in which we all
live. Some will come because of the selfishness and evil of
humanity. But regardless of their origin, know that God will
not waste any of them. He will redeem it all, and if you cooperate with Him, He will use your experiences in the valley
to help grow and shape you. Ultimately, He will use those
experiences to prepare you for eternity.

Your valley will have moments of laughter and joy beyond measure. Your valley will be filled with accomplish-
ments and rewarding experiences. Your valley will be filled
with the occasional trip to the mountaintop. Some of those
mountaintop experiences may include weddings, celebrations, dream vacations, retirement, awards, or when your
child or favorite team wins the game on a last-second shot
or touchdown. Some of your mountaintop experiences will
be grand. Some will be simple. But if you let them, each

mountaintop experience will give you the proper perspective of your valley. Each mountaintop experience will remind you again of the wonder that abounds in your valley.

Your valley will consist mostly of the simple. There will be chores and work. There will be crumbs to wipe up, dishes to clean, and floors to vacuum. There will be grass to mow and leaves to rake. There will be school assemblies, camps, sporting events, birthday parties, and the occasional vacation. Elementary as the valley may seem, it is far from it. Do not miss the wonder of your routine. You are not passing through these moments randomly. They are God's gift to you, on purpose. With the proper perspective, your simplicity has incredible potential. Do not take it for granted. Stop and behold the wonder of the routine. This is your valley, perfectly designed for you, and it has incredible beauty.

Your valley will also consist of loss. There will be death. No one escapes it. There is a time for each of us. There will be tears, and you will feel an emptiness that seems as deep as a bottomless pit. You will grieve, but if you walk with the Lord, you will not grieve without hope. The Scriptures tell us in 1 Thessalonians 4:13-14 (NLT), "We want you to know what will happen to the believers who have died so you will not grieve like people who have no hope. For since we believe that Jesus died and was raised to life again, we also

> We want you to know what will happen to the believers who have died so you will not grieve like people who have no hope. For since we believe that Jesus died and was raised to life again, we also believe that when Jesus returns, God will bring back with him the believers who have died.
>
> 1 THESSALONIANS 4:13-14

believe that when Jesus returns, God will bring back with him the believers who have died."

Remember also the words of the Lord in Psalm 23:4 (KJV): "Though I walk through the valley of the shadow of death...thou art with me." This will be one of the greatest lessons the valley will teach you. The "valley of the shadow of death" is something we walk through. As we walk, the Lord walks with us every step of the way. That valley is not a place where God leaves us stranded. God is walking you "through the valley." He is taking you somewhere. Your valley is ultimately not your home. If you know God, eternity is your home. Your valley is not the destination; it is only the preparation for your ultimate destination—heaven. Strangely and beautifully, the only way you get there is through the valley of the shadow of death.

If there is anything your valley will tell you, it is that everything that takes place in the valley is doing something to prepare you for your eternal home. So, keep moving and surrendering it all to the Lord.

Your valley is taking you up to the ultimate mountain. In the book of Hebrews 12:22, the Scriptures call it "Mount Zion, the city of the living God, the heavenly Jerusalem." It is here that you will be reunited in eternity with the loved ones you miss who walked with the Lord as well. It is here that you will have the ultimate mountaintop experience forever. It is here that you will have the ultimate perspective. It is here where everything will finally make sense. It is here that you will see how beautiful and purposeful your valley was intended to be—every single second of it. It is here that you will see how much living and growth took place in your valley, especially the hard parts. Every routine second had divine purpose, even when you couldn't see it or feel it. Oh, the wonder of the valley!

1 Corinthians 13:12 (NLT) describes that moment this way: "Now we see things imperfectly, like puzzling reflections

in a mirror, but then we will see everything with perfect clarity. All that I know now is partial and incomplete, but then I will know everything completely, just as God knows me completely."

It was time to end our family mountaintop experience and begin the hike back down to the valley. In all the times before this one, I always hated leaving the top of the mountain. It was difficult to end the experience. But this time, it was different, as have been all the mountaintop experiences since.

I began to walk with my family down the trail littered with jagged rocks and tree roots. Our mountaintop experience had been a great one. But down in the valley, there was a minivan waiting. There were crumbs to wipe, things to clean, practices to attend, daily tasks and assignments to complete, and multiple routine duties and events ahead. I looked back at the mountaintop, thankful for the perspective. I turned and began to make the joyful journey to the bottom.

As I walked, I was bursting with thankfulness. Below, there was a valley filled with opportunities for growth, beauty, and wonder. There was a valley below, and it was pointing me to eternity, the ultimate ascension.

> Now we see things imperfectly, like puzzling reflections in a mirror, but then we will see everything with perfect clarity. All that I know now is partial and incomplete, but then I will know everything completely, just as God knows me completely.
>
> 1 CORINTHIANS 13:12

Christmas

27

Staying In The Moment

It was the evening of December 25, 2021. The Christmas rush had come and gone as quickly as an Appalachian storm. The floors and couches of our living room were littered with wrapping paper and long-awaited, brand-new gifts. They bore witness to the unbridled joy that filled the room just hours before. Each torn sheet and piece of tissue served as a monumental tapestry to laughter, bliss, wonder, family ties, hopeful expectations met, and even a few unmet expectations.

Andy Rooney's quote, "One of the most glorious messes in the world is the mess created in the living room on Christmas day. Don't clean it up too quickly." is as true as it sounds. Our living room was brimming with Christmas mess, and it was perfectly beautiful. I still contend that our couches look much better with toys and clothes from Christmas draped across them. It doesn't leave much room for sitting, but the sight, memories, and moments that accompany them make it all worth standing or sitting on the floor.

As usual on the night of Christmas day, my eyes were weary and my body was fatigued. The days before Christmas have always been joyously sleepless for me. There is simply too much to be awake for during this time period. I find myself not wanting to miss a moment of it. In the peace of this post-Christmas moment, I stood viewing this beautiful mess, as I do each year, and I was thankful to God for it.

Just as the peace of this moment began to engulf me, my youngest son, Baylon, walked into the room. He stood at the foot of the wood-stained entertainment center that housed so many of our Christmas decorations each year and looked straight up at the elf perched at the top, dead center.

The "Elf on the Shelf" is a Christmas tradition we have employed with our boys since they were all young. Each night during the Christmas season, the elf moves to a different location in the house, leaving everyone to wake up wondering where he or she has landed. It is a tradition that gives a great opportunity for creativity. Sadly, the tradition loses its momentum as your kids grow older. The effort to keep it alive takes creativity and fortitude. Though it has lost some of its momentum with my two older boys, it had not yet lost its momentum with my then 12-year-old.

Traditionally, all elves return to the North Pole on Christmas Eve. But for the last two years, Baylon had asked for an extra day. The North Pole had gladly granted the request. The extra 24 hours were over, and it was time for the elf to make his leave until next year. Baylon made his way into the middle of the Christmas living room mess and stood before the elf. The elf had left a special note reminding Baylon to "stay a kid." While this was not going to be possible physically, it could certainly be done in his heart.

I was not naïve; I realized my youngest son was at the moment of his life when he was seemingly suspended between two realities. Childhood belief, wonder, and imagination were beckoning and begging him not to leave. Adolescence was crowding its way in and commanding its place in line, waiting to usher him into adulthood.

As a parent, I watched this happen, trying to navigate the process accurately. Secretly, I hoped that childhood wonder would win this tug-of-war. But I knew adolescence and adulthood would have their day, as they should. So, I turned my energies to the fight for keeping wonder tucked away in his heart forever. The fight is difficult and emotional but worth the effort.

I was left with this one little, unexpected, marvelous moment that invited itself into my space on Christmas Day 2021. I was not surprised. Thankfully, I was completely aware of it and had the sense to welcome it. My youngest kid, about to turn a teenager, raised up his arm above his head, waved at the elf, and said, "Goodbye, elf, see you next year." As tears began to flow from my eyes, I wondered if he was just saying goodbye to the elf or also unconsciously saying goodbye to his childhood. Maybe it was both.

> I turned my energies to the fight for keeping wonder tucked away in his heart.

It seemed a page was turning from one chapter to another. The tears continued to flow, but I didn't fight them.

Too many miraculous moments come into our lives disguised as routine. They make their invitation wrapped in the mundane, and we fail to give them entry due to what we deem as insignificance. We are too quick to clean up the clutter, too busy to stop or wait, and too rushed to get to the next big thing or the next big moment. We have to get here or get over there.

Sure, there is a time to move forward and move on. But it's also important to recognize that we all live one second from eternity. Not a moment of extra time is guaranteed to us. Knowing this should give us pause to embrace the significance of small things. Every moment we experience could be our last. We should not rush ourselves out of those moments.

I walked over and put my arm around Baylon's shoulders. We both looked at the elf, realizing that right in the middle of that beautiful mess and clutter, the extraordinary had stepped in and overtaken the ordinary. To many, the moment would seem quite routine, mundane, or insignificant. But to us, it was so much more than that. Words were fittingly left unspoken. We did not rush the moment nor rush to exit it. We just stood and embraced it. The moment was monumental for me because I knew we would not have it again. I wasn't sure if he'd ever look at the elf that way again.

When we position ourselves for these moments, we find that life is much more extraordinary than it seems. Miraculous moments of wonder are wading through every conventional and periodic mess of life, waiting to be experienced and give firm footings to our faith. When these seemingly insignificant yet miraculous moments invite themselves into the clutter of your routine, always give a warm welcome, pull up a chair, and embrace them. You never know which one may be your last.

> Too many miraculous moments come into our lives disguised as routine. We are too quick to clean up the clutter.

28

My Pivotal Christmas

December 24, 1984. That was my pivotal Christmas. That was the year I came to an intersection in my life about Christmas, faith, and belief. It happened at the crossroads of the epic, transitional turn from childhood to adulthood. Much of how I view Christmas today was strewn about in pieces in the middle of that intersection that night. I wasn't aware of it then, but the choice I made while lying in my bed that Christmas Eve impacts my life to this day. It happened this way.

On Christmas Eve 1984, I laid completely soundless in my bed, covers pulled up over my ears. I had one eye open and one shut. I tried desperately to force myself to sleep. The clock read 12:07 a.m. There would be no sleep to rescue me. Perhaps the covers pulled over my head would deafen the blusterous, heavy-handed sound I did not want to hear. But to no avail. My mother and father had hurriedly ushered me to sleep. "Now, go to sleep. Santa has to come, and he gets tired easy these days." The lack of subtlety in their words offered me little hope. Perhaps they thought I had come to

> I would not let it be just another month or holiday. I chose faith, belief, and wonder.

terms with what I had refused to as a brand-new adolescent. With that statement and the lights of the house still beaming through the bottom of my closed door, the last little bit of hope I had left was slowly leaking out of my heart.

All of a sudden, 12:17 a.m.—a reprieve! Out of nowhere, at the bottom of my door, two giant feet appeared, bursting their shadows through the bottom of my door as they were backlit by the light in my parents' bedroom. They moved ever so slowly toward the door. The doorknob turned, and the door cracked open. Could it be!? I closed my eyes and breathed heavily to give the appearance of deep sleep. My parents' words every Christmas Eve began to ring through my head. "If you're not asleep, Santa won't come!" I sensed a figure of some sort standing in my room. As the figure exited, I turned quickly to look. Shatteringly, hope blown, I saw the back of my mom as she walked out the door.

> Santa isn't the center of the story. The truth of the Savior is the center of the story.

The next thing I heard was the closet door open in my parent's bedroom. I heard the ruffling of paper bags. I watched footsteps scamper back and forth across the shadow of my closed bedroom door into the place where Santa always left our gifts around the Christmas tree. There seemed to be no effort of covertness.

At that moment, my heart sank into the pit of my stomach, and my throat began to lump. The warmth of the salty tear rolling down my cheek broke apart the cold December chill in the room. I desperately wanted all my friends to be wrong. Christmas didn't seem to be epic to them anymore. They had already made the turn at the intersection and left me behind. Even in the uncertainty of this moment, I refused to follow them. They listened to rap and pop music at Christmas. I still listened to Bing Crosby and watched

Rudolph the Red-Nosed Reindeer. I refused. I would not let it be just another month or holiday. I found myself at the intersection everyone had always talked about, but I didn't want to believe it.

Strangely, I knew how epic this moment was that lay before me. The direction I went from this extraordinary moment would determine more than just Christmas from this day forward; it would determine everything. I knew that if I went one way, Christmas would go from color to black and white. I would never listen to Christmas music the same way; I would never see Christmas decorations the same way; I would never anticipate the rush of the season the same way. Christmas Eve would never be the same. But most of all, I would leave wonder in the dust, and I would march to the same humdrum beat as the rest of society. I refused to go the way my friends had gone.

> Behold, I bring you good news of great joy that will be for all the people. For unto you is born this day in the city of David a Savior, who is Christ the Lord.
>
> LUKE 2:10-11

The choice was still mine. It was a difficult choice, but it was also strangely beautiful and perfect. I had dreaded this day and moment. I had fought it. I wanted things to continue as I had always known them. But the fight for wonder and joy was before me, and in spite of any misperceived disappointment, the fight was worth it. Lying on my bed that Christmas Eve, I chose faith, belief, and wonder. I would not let the world steal them from me.

You may ask, "Yeah, but what about the whole Santa thing?" That night, I realized Santa was more real than he had ever been before. He was more than a fat, jolly old elf who rides the night skies delivering presents on Christmas Eve. He wasn't merely a man in a red suit as I had always thought him to be, growing up as a child. Santa was a posture; he was a frame of mind; he was a way of thinking and acting. He represented sacrifice, saving, giving, joy, selflessness, and yes, even wonder. Santa didn't stop existing for me that night; I just discovered his true identity. In many ways, he was even better than I had imagined.

To this day, my mother or father have never said anything to me about the reality (or not) of Santa. They've always said, "I believe." That's enough for me. That Christmas Eve, I was not mad at them. I was just grateful for every Christmas Eve I had had as a child—every sacrifice, every saved penny, and every magical moment.

On Christmas Eve in 1984, I realized how inconsequential Santa was to the whole Christmas story. Sure, he's one small part of all the joy around it, and I'm thankful for that. But Santa isn't the center of the story. The truth of the Savior is the center of the story, and that is anything but fantasy; that is eternal truth.

That night, in choosing wonder, I knew I was choosing a faithful disposition of joy and wonder for what is and what is to come. I was choosing to rise above disappointment. I was choosing to be faithful in the midst of the stark reality of difficulty. I was choosing to see things that I couldn't see with my naked eye. For the first time, I think I fully understood the pronouncement of

> When troubles of any kind come your way, consider it an opportunity for great joy. For you know that when your faith is tested, your endurance has a chance to grow. So let it grow, for when your endurance is fully developed, you will be perfect and complete, needing nothing.
>
> JAMES 1:2-3

the angel in Luke 2:10-11 (ESV), "Behold, I bring you good news of great joy that will be for all the people. For unto you is born this day in the city of David a Savior, who is Christ the Lord."

That wasn't a statement measuring the current conditions; it was a pronouncement of hope that is here and still to come. It was a pronouncement that all of this is going somewhere. There will always be difficulty. There will always be struggles in this broken world. There will always be intersections filled with cold, hard realities. But at every intersection, there is a choice. The choice will determine how vividly you see and hear the melody of this temporary life that leads to glory, most certainly for those who have faith in Christ.

> These troubles...produce for us a glory that vastly outweighs them and will last forever...so we fix our gaze on things that cannot be seen.
>
> 2 CORINTHIANS 4:17-18

James 1:2-3 (NLT) says, "When troubles of any kind come your way, consider it an opportunity for great joy. For you know that when your faith is tested, your endurance has a chance to grow. So let it grow, for when your endurance is fully developed, you will be perfect and complete, needing nothing."

That Christmas Eve in 1984, troubles came my way, and I stood at the intersection called "opportunity for joy;" I chose joy. Santa was the catalyst. Who knew? Since that night, troubles much bigger than that crisis of belief have invaded my life. I'm still choosing the Lord's opportunities for joy amid the difficulty.

As the Apostle Paul wrote in 2 Corinthians 4:17-18 (NLT), "These troubles...produce for us a glory that vastly outweighs them and will last forever...so we fix our gaze on things that cannot be seen." That's choosing faith; that's choosing wonder; that's choosing joy. Because it's the things you can't see yet that will end up being the most real things.

Choose joy and wonder. No matter how difficult it may be, choose them! Choose to see with the eyes of faith. That choice will lead you to something far greater than a room full of presents on Christmas Day, it will lead you to God's glorious presence for all eternity.

29
Picture Perfect

The picture you see here is from Christmas Day 2014. It looks almost picture-perfect. It gives the appearance of a perfect, well-put-together family Christmas. It gives the appearance of one of those ideal Christmas moments. It gives the appearance of Christmas Wonder in full effect. But this picture is rooted in chaos. It took effort and time to get this picture. It took effort and timing to get rid of the tears, hurt, and disorder that occurred before the picture was taken.

We have a tradition in our house that has taken place since my boys were young kids and still carries on to this day. On Christmas Day morning, the boys and I gather in one of their bedrooms at the end of the hallway in our house. It is still dark outside, and the sun hasn't even thought about coming up yet. Candles in the window are the only things that give light to the room. Christmas tree lights illuminate down the hallway to give an added ray of magical light. The setting is Christmas, holy and perfect. We then read the story of the birth of Jesus from Luke 2 in the Bible. We follow that with worship to Jesus and close by singing "Happy Birthday" to Jesus. We put first things first.

Once that is done, I retreat into the family room, where Santa has left all their gifts in their prospective places. My wife prepares the camera; I prepare the video. I proceed to play the "Hallelujah Chorus" through the loudspeaker in the house. We then release the boys to make the mad dash down the hallway to see what Santa has left them! And yes, they still make the mad dash with as much excitement as they did when they were younger! It is a sight to behold and one of the highlights of the year.

Christmas Day 2014 was no different. We had gone through all the "first things first," holy moments. Attitudes were in check, perspectives were right, and all was well. Christmas Day and its moments were shaping up to be another memorable experience in the Carnes household. The boys had gathered at the end of the hallway. They began jumping up and down. Excitement was in the air. The "Hallelujah Chorus" began with its usual zest and vibrant joy. I released the boys!

They came together, pummeling down the hall. They only needed to make the left turn into the family room. All of a sudden, my middle son, Ryder, who had been pulling up the rear behind his brothers Baylon and Jadon, in great Nascar form, took an inside route, stuck out his elbow, slammed Baylon into the wall, and moved out front. Baylon hit the wall and, in true five-year-old fashion, fell to the ground and began to scream and cry as if a tiger had bitten off his foot. Yes, he overplayed it, but the drama and chaos ruined the perfection of the moment.

Everything was now in disarray. I immediately stopped the moment. I stopped the tape, stopped the camera, halted the other two boys, and told all three to get back to the room. We couldn't have all that screaming and drama on the camera roll. It wouldn't play out well in the memory log. I sent them all back down the hallway. No presents, no gifts, no Santa. My oldest son Jadon yelled out, "Ryder, you ruined Christmas!" Ryder began to cry. Baylon was still crying. Jadon was screaming, and I was overreacting to it all. We had gone from Christmas holiness to complete Southern dysfunction in a matter of minutes. All the while, my wife stood in shock and speechless, camera in hand in the hallway. I was angry because our Christmas perfection had been tainted.

I won't bore anyone with the specifics of everything that was said. But apologies were made (including my own for overreacting and getting angry), tears were shed, hugs were given, and forgiveness was offered. Humorously, we even felt like we needed to sing a few songs to Jesus again. The boys lined up again with a promise not to slam each other into the hallway. I promised not to get mad, and the boys began to laugh and be joyful again. The "Hallelujah Chorus" began again. *Joy!* We got a second chance. Thank you, Lord!

Though it seemed chaotic in the moment, I think back to that moment with fondness and much gratitude. It is one of the Christmas memories I remember most. Why? Not because it was peaceful, with the perfect set of circumstances, but because we found peace in the midst of the imperfection.

Though we long for the perfect Christmas and try to produce perfect Christmas moments every year, the truth is that the real essence of Christmas is about finding peace in the midst of the chaos. It's about knowing that in spite of less-than-ideal circumstances, there is still *joy* that is bigger than all of it and reigning over all.

We've fancied Christmas as some sort of picture-perfect postcard, but it was anything but that. There was no room for the young parents of Jesus. There was scandal and there were accusations. There was a dark and cold feeding trough for animals. There were dirty shepherds. The world was dark, without hope, and under the rule of tyranny. There were threats against the child's life. Chaos was everywhere.

But against that backdrop, the angels broke through the night sky with a message of good news to all that Hope was born! The skies lit up with life and salvation, and a second chance was born! In that moment of less-than-ideal, peace and joy came to form. But make no mistake, the child was born to die. The soft hands and gentle cooing would give way to bloodied, nail-scarred hands and the cry of "Father, forgive them, for they know not what they do." In that moment of less-than-ideal, peace and joy came to form.

Philippians 4:6-7 (NLT) says, "Don't worry about anything; instead, pray about everything. Tell God what you need, and thank him for all he has done. Then you will experience God's peace, which exceeds anything we can understand. His peace will guard your hearts and minds as you live in Christ Jesus."

It is profound that God never dismisses chaos or imperfection. But He does promise peace and triumph through it and in the midst of it. The same is true today. No matter how much you decorate them, ERs are still ERs. Funeral homes are still funeral homes. No amount of garland can shape a hospice house into perfect Christmas form. The chaos of life can be filled with more a tear than cheer. Yet, that is where Christmas is generally found most profoundly. Somewhere down in the midst of the imperfection is a peace unexplainable.

> Don't worry about anything; instead, pray about everything. Tell God what you need, and thank him for all he has done. Then you will experience God's peace, which exceeds anything we can understand. His peace will guard your hearts and minds as you live in Christ Jesus.
>
> PHILIPPIANS 4:6-7

I deleted that imperfect video that day. It is one of my biggest regrets. We always try to erase and avoid the imperfect things, don't we? Had I kept it, I would have seen that my family was given a second-chance moment, not only in the midst of the imperfection but because of it. But the memory still burns in my heart, and it's not going anywhere.

Christmas is a profound reminder that God was victorious even in a world of hopelessness, tyrannical rule and government, an overcrowded inn, scandalous assumptions about an untimely pregnancy, ordinary people, and mundane, less-than-ideal circumstances.

> God never dismisses chaos or imperfection. He is victorious in my imperfections and less-than-ideal circumstances.

God is victorious in my imperfections and less-than-ideal circumstances. Strangely, in the midst of my less-than-perfect, mundane reality, I feel peace and wonder. The peace and wonder make their way into the crevices of my heart, not in spite of the imperfections but in many ways because of them. God has a beautiful way of working in such a fashion.

30

Make Room For The Left Turn

Every Christmas, when my family is on the way home from an event in town, there is the option to take a left turn into a neighborhood. In that neighborhood is a house that rivals any Christmas lighting display I have ever seen. It is grand and spectacular. The trees in this yard are littered with lights. The house is covered with lights. The grass, the driveway, the steps, every single component of this domicile is filled with a marvelous display of Christmas decorations and lights. There are metal trusses crossing the yard, and other exterior structures that heighten and lend to the grandiose nature of the scene. All of the lights are timed and in sync, and a sign directs you to a particular station that plays Christmas music for the background and dancing show of lights. The owners of this property begin decorating mid to late Summer. It takes that long to prepare.

He missed out on something he needed more than the path of least resistance.

Every year, particularly when my kids were younger, they would scream and cry out, "Let's go by the house with the lights! Make the left turn!" It has become a tradition.

The left turn crosses oncoming traffic. On the way out of the neighborhood, you must make another left turn across two lanes of traffic. The turn requires skill and attention. The trip requires effort. I will confess there are some moments where, out of expedience, I have considered refusing the turn and the trip, desiring to claim busyness or fatigue as an excuse. But every time I've made the turn, I've never regretted the experience, and I've always been glad that I made the effort. It has always been worth it. As a result, I have never refused it and always held the door open.

The Bible tells us in Luke 2:6-7 (NLT), "And while they were there, the time came for her baby to be born. She gave birth to her firstborn son. She wrapped him snugly in strips of cloth and laid him in a manger, because there was no lodging available for them."

When it comes to the story of the birth of Jesus, we get very little information about the Innkeeper. But he always has a place in most Nativity recreations at Christmas. We really don't even know if there was an Innkeeper. We generally assume there was an Innkeeper, and it's likely there was one.

When the little town of Bethlehem became a metropolis for hustle and bustle due to a census, the "Inn" business had to be booming, with so many people arriving in town. As a result, there was money to be made.

> And while they were there, the time came for her baby to be born. She gave birth to her firstborn son. She wrapped him snugly in strips of cloth and laid him in a manger, because there was no lodging available for them.
>
> LUKE 2:6-7

No one would have left their Inn unattended. So someone had to tell Mary and Joseph there was no room left. Hence, we get the Innkeeper. While we get little to no information about him, what we do know is that if he truly existed, he turned Mary and Joseph away. He told them there was no room. He refused to open the door or make the turn.

The Bible tells us there was no room, but let's be real for a moment. There was a young expectant mother who was about to have a baby, and she was desperate. Wouldn't you make room for a mother-to-be? Maybe it was too late. Maybe he was too tired. Maybe it would have required too much work. Maybe a pregnant woman giving birth to a baby in the middle of the night would have been quite unsettling to all the other guests at the Inn, causing a backlash the Innkeeper would prefer to avoid. Perhaps they had no money to offer him. Perhaps there was nothing to be gained for the trouble.

> Behind every moment that threatens to overwhelm or stress us, there is a gentle Savior, knocking, and waiting for an opportunity. Choose the wonder.

If only someone would have clued the Innkeeper in to the fact that this child was the King of kings and Lord of lords, the One who had come to die and be raised to life for his salvation. Odds are very high there would have all of a sudden been room. But Isaiah 53 reminds us that Jesus came and there was "nothing to attract us to him... there was nothing beautiful or majestic about his appearance." No fanfare, no majestic announcement, only a subtle knock. But as a result, it produced no effort on the part of the Innkeeper. The knock was subtle, without pomp and circumstance, but behind it was an incredible opportunity. The Innkeeper refused the opportunity, and he missed out on something he needed more than the path of least resistance. There are many who still choose the path of least resistance, and they miss the opportunity as well.

From an eternal perspective, December is no more special than June, particularly when you carry Jesus in your heart all year long. But the reason I love Christmas so much is because it seems as though the rest of the world is more open to opportunity, to opening doors, and making left turns. As a result, though they are present and available all year long, things like joy, wonder, and awe seem to come to the forefront in December. But just as they were for the Innkeeper, all of these things carry a choice with them.

Jesus said in Revelation 3:20 (ESV), "Behold, I stand at the door and knock. If you hear my voice and open the door, I will come in." It's interesting to me that the first door Jesus ever knocked on in this world, even while He was still in the womb, was shut in his face. Since then, millions upon millions of people have made a choice to open the door, and they have not regretted it. I am one of them.

> Behold, I stand at the door and knock. If you hear my voice and open the door, I will come in.
>
> REVELATION 3:20

Each year, Christmas will call upon our hearts and march into our lives. Christmas is busy. Life is busy. There will be parties, family gatherings, shopping, events and programs. We will be tired and overwhelmed at times. There will even be depression, anxiety, and grief for some. Don't let the moments overwhelm you. Embrace them. Behind every moment that threatens to overwhelm or stress us, there is a gentle Savior, knocking, and waiting for an opportunity. He is gentle, He will not force Himself upon you. You will have to make the effort to step out of the traffic. You will have to choose the wonder. You will have to make the left turn. You may have to cross oncoming traffic, but the effort will be worth it, and you won't regret it. You have to make room.

Take the left turn, drive by the lights, walk through the mall, make the effort to show up for worship, breathe it all in. He is knocking, there are incredible opportunities to be had. Prepare yourself, make room, take the left turn. You won't regret it. That thing you thought you couldn't muster up the strength to do or had time to do, could just be holding the one thing you need most. Make room.

Perspective

31
Crumbs

Day after day, morning and night, I wipe away these crumbs. I wipe them off the stovetop. I wipe them off the kitchen counter. I wipe them off the dining room table. I sweep them off the hardwood floor of the kitchen. I sweep them off the hardwood floor of the dining room. Over and over, again and again, I wipe and I sweep these crumbs. It has become part of my daily life and routine. I complete the task for one day, only to repeat it again the next. Awake, eat, wipe and sweep crumbs. Come home, eat, wipe and sweep crumbs, go to bed, repeat. It is part of my routine. I have been continuously repeating this operation for over twenty years, since the birth of my first child.

I have attempted to train each of my three boys in the glorious duty of wiping and sweeping away crumbs. Not only have I trained them, but I have given them the assignment. This has become their daily chore. "Hold your food over your plate. Pick up after yourself. Make sure you wipe off the table. Sweep under the chairs. Do it again." The boys have accepted the assignment with little resistance. Unfortunately, they have yet to perform it with any amount of enthusiasm, detail, or quality.

As a result, my wiping up and sweeping crumbs has evolved into wiping and sweeping away the crumbs my boys missed on their initial, repeated attempts to wipe and sweep. That process has also become a repetitious daily cycle in my life. Until I am able to fully raise the standard of their performance, it will continue to be my repetitious daily cycle.

It would be easy to assume that I grow tired and weary of this seemingly never-ending task. It would be easy to assume that after twenty years of this daily routine, my posture toward it may become fatigued or that I would long for its end. But nothing could be further from the truth. Honestly, there will be a day when it will end, and I will be sad. I will miss it. What could cause such endearment to a tiresome daily chore? The answer is simple: perspective.

It's not what you look at that matters; it's what you see.

To many, the crumbs may appear to be the signal of another boring task. To many, the crumbs may give the sign of untidiness. To me, they are the sight of something beautiful. They are the reminder of something marvelous. Little things are not little. It's not what you look at that matters; it's what you see.

The moments before the crumbs appear have been filled with moments of laughter and fellowship. The moments before the crumbs appear are filled with three boys and two parents sharing love and togetherness. The moments before the crumbs appear are filled with talks about school experiences. They are filled with talks about sports and practices. They are filled with talks about relationships and girlfriends. They are filled with jokes. These moments are teaching moments. These moments are filled with watching my boys fill their stomachs, receive sustenance, and be thankful for it. Love and affection bring me these moments before the crumbs appear, and I am thankful.

In a world where so many go to bed hungry each night, these crumbs are the reminder that I have more than I deserve. The crumbs remind me that my pantry is full of food. Not only is the pantry full of food, but it is full of choices and options for food. Who are we to eat like such kings? The crumbs are a reminder that there shall be no room for complaints or ingratitude in this household.

The crumbs remind me that we have utensils and equipment upon which to prepare and cook the food. We have the resources to power the equipment to cook the food, and all of it comes on demand with the simple turn of a knob. There is no rummaging the forest for sticks or trying to find fire for cooking.

The crumbs remind me that we sit at a table in a home with a roof over our heads. The home is temperature-controlled. We can heat and cool it on demand. We don't sit on street corners as many less fortunate in the world are forced to do. The crumbs remind me that we eat with utensils and not our hands. The crumbs remind me that we have running water coming out of a faucet with which to wash the food down and away—all on demand with the turn of a knob.

The crumbs remind me that we have the towels and equipment to wipe and sweep them away. The crumbs remind me that God provides all of these tools, towels, equipment, and resources. This is the same God who gives my wife and me the gifts and opportunities to labor and work with our hands and minds. This work helps to bring in the income needed to provide for our daily needs. We work, labor, and try to provide as best we can. It may not be much, but it's always enough. This is a gift. Many are unable to work. Many are unable to provide. The crumbs remind me to give to those who have less. The crumbs remind me to do all that I can to serve the less fortunate.

The crumbs remind me that we have food to eat, a house in which to live, and most of all, a family to love and with which to share life.

The crumbs are a reminder that every meal that produces them is preceded by a prayer. This prayer is the one that we use to thank God for each other, for this moment, and for what He has given us. When I wipe away the crumbs, I remember the prayer, and I thank God for the crumbs and everything that comes with them, before them, and after them. The crumbs point me to the promise of Jesus in Matthew 6:32b-34 (NLT): "But your heavenly Father already knows all your needs. Seek the Kingdom of God above all else, and live righteously, and he will give you everything you need. So don't worry about tomorrow, for tomorrow will bring its own worries. Today's trouble is enough for today."

In a world filled with worry and anxiety, perhaps the simple process of wiping and sweeping away crumbs is the best medication. The Lord will provide, so seek Him first. You are still here, even as hard as things may seem. He is not finished with you yet. Keep Him first. When He is done with you, He will bring you to be with Him in His perfect timing. Until then, keep wiping, keep sweeping, keep going, and stay thankful.

The crumbs keep me humble. The crumbs put my daily events into proper perspective. They remind me that I

> But your heavenly Father already knows all your needs. Seek the Kingdom of God above all else, and live righteously, and he will give you everything you need. So don't worry about tomorrow, for tomorrow will bring its own worries. Today's trouble is enough for today.
>
> MATTHEW 6:32B-34

am not the king. The crumbs remind me that no task is too small, too little, or too menial for my attention or service. The crumbs remind me that I am called to love and serve. The crumbs remind me that there is a beauty in living simply and quietly. The crumbs remind me that there is a grand adventure in every mundane, routine part of my day.

Perhaps one day, the table will be filled with grandchildren, and there will be more crumbs to wipe and sweep. I will embrace it, even if my aged body does not. One day, my boys will be wiping away crumbs of their own in their own houses. I will teach them to embrace the wiping and sweeping away of every crumb.

Inevitably, if I am blessed to live that long, the boys will leave the house and go out on their own. One day, our table will be filled with fewer people. One day, it may just be my wife and I again. One day, I will miss the wiping and sweeping away of crumbs.

Little things are never little.

One day, there may only be my crumbs to wipe up, as I sit at the table alone. If that happens, I will not forget the lessons forged in the wiping and sweeping away of crumbs, and I will be thankful for that season. I hope and pray in that moment that I will also find the beauty and gratitude in the wiping and sweeping away of my own crumbs. God's faithfulness will not have changed, even in that moment of solitude and isolation.

So, I wipe and sweep, day after day, morning and night, crumb after crumb. My daily routine awaits me. It is beautiful and filled with wonder. It is filled with life lessons. It is filled with opportunities to be humbled and to serve. It is also littered with reminders of God's grace, care, and provision. If you see a tear flowing down my face while wiping and sweeping away the crumbs, just know that they are not tears of sadness. They are tears that point to a wonderful discovery: the wonder of the routine and all its reminders.

Little things are never little. It's not what you look at that matters; it's what you see. In those crumbs and in the glory of my routine, I see quite a bit. Thank you for the reminder, Lord.

32

O The Blood

"**W**anting to release Jesus, Pilate appealed to them again. But they kept shouting, 'Crucify him! Crucify him!'" (Luke 23:20)

Just a few days earlier, they were all shouting, "Hosanna! Hosanna! Blessed is he who comes in the name of the Lord." What happened? They didn't get the version of Jesus they wanted, so they turned on Him. O the blood of Jesus.

So often, we do the same thing. We tend to try to twist Scripture and twist Jesus into the version that suits our life choices; then, like so many who experienced all the events of that week, we end up speaking out of both sides of our mouths. O the blood of Jesus.

Their praises were so loud and passionate that day that even Jesus said, "If they keep quiet, the stones will cry out."

O the blood of Jesus.

Tragically and strangely, they were now furiously calling for the execution of the very One they had praised so passionately a few days earlier. Their shouts prevailed. "But with loud shouts, they insistently demanded that he be crucified, and their shouts prevailed." (Luke 23:23) O the blood of Jesus.

Fittingly, the same Jesus who did not suppress their shouting praises did not suppress their shouts for his death either. It is because this is what He came to do. He came to die for the very ones who had both praised Him and called for His execution. He came to die for the many who had led such duplicitous lifestyles, for the ones who had spoken out of both sides of their mouths, the ones who had so often said one thing, and done a different thing. I know, I've been one of them. O the blood of Jesus.

Remember the beautiful and peaceful manger scene at Christmas? Remember singing "Away in A Manger"? Remember the moment the Wise Men walked in with the three gifts? One of those gifts was myrrh, a liquid used to embalm the dead. This moment on the cross is what that gift signaled. The beauty of that scene was intended to give way to the horror and brutality of the scene at the cross. "Away in a Manger" was meant to give way to "When I Survey the Wondrous Cross." O the blood of Jesus.

I have been the recipient of His grace and mercy, and have gotten way more from Jesus than I ever deserved.

When He hung on that cross, with all the people at his feet still ridiculing and sneering Him, Jesus lovingly and amazingly spoke the words, "Father, forgive them, for they do not know what they are doing." (Luke 23:34) But Jesus knew exactly what He was doing. He was dying to save their sins. Only a few days later, He would rise from the dead to offer them salvation and forgiveness. O the blood of Jesus.

I have spoken out of both sides of my mouth. I have said one thing and done another. I have tried to twist Jesus to suit my personal convictions and life choices, rather than taking up my own cross and following Him on the path of truth and suffering, even when it hurts and means I don't always get what I desire. O the blood of Jesus.

In all of that, I have also been on the other end of "Father forgive them, for they do not know what they are doing" more times than I can count. I have been the recipient of His grace and mercy, and have gotten way more from Jesus than I ever deserved. I am the wretch the song talks about. But I also got "Amazing Grace." And that is why I go to my knees each and every day, and proclaim...O the blood of Jesus.

33

The Happy Place

It was a textbook beach day. The sky was a deep, textured blue with thin layers of white clouds stretched like spider webs. The breeze was slight, not enough to be annoying but just enough to offer refreshment. The ocean had a perfect turquoise, opaque glow. The warm sun beaming down only made it brighter. Coastal saltiness scented the air perfectly. The song of the seagulls brought a brightening melody to the ear. The crash of the waves, followed by the ripple of the current, would be the perfect sound effect for deep sleep. The cool tide washing slowly over my outstretched feet provided the sublime garnish to the day. My wife was beside me, my kids were frolicking in the ocean before me, and the cares of the world were behind me. It was an impeccable setting.

A "happy place" could never be reduced to a geographical location, time period, or set of circumstances.

This would be the moment for the obligatory snapshot of my feet resting on the sand with the ocean before me that so many take and post on social media, along with the words, "My happy place." It would have fit nicely. It was a place, and it made me happy. Strangely, I resisted the urge. I resisted because, at that moment when all of my external circumstances seemed faultless, something began to wash over me other than the rippling current of the Atlantic.

As I watched my kids laugh, play, wrestle, ride the waves, scream, and smile, I began to get tunnel vision. It was as if the beauty of the ocean, the sand, the perfect sky, and the crashing waves all went black, and the only thing I could see were my children. In seconds, I pictured all of the ball games, Christmas Eve's past, plays, musicals, bike rides, first and last days of school, struggles, fights, life lessons, and so much more. I was reduced to tears, not because of sadness but because of joy. I was awash in the realization that a "happy place" could never be reduced to a geographical location, time period, or set of circumstances.

> I have come that they may have life, and that they may have it more abundantly.
>
> JOHN 10:10

To be clear, I understand what most people mean when they refer to their "happy place." There are places that make us happier than other places. I understand that many will retire or move to a geographical place they like better than others. I understand that most people don't literally mean that if they're not constantly in a certain geographical location with a certain set of circumstances, they can never be happy.

If only life could be so simple and easy that a "happy place" was a geographical location. Then, we could send all the broken marriages and families there, and everything would be spared. We could send all the addicts there, and they could be free. We could send all the angry, the displaced, the broken, and the dysfunctional there, and everything could be made right. Not so much. Why didn't God create a beach or range of mountains on every street corner if this were true? Sadly, even beaches and mountains have homeless, broken, addicted, divorced, orphaned, and marginal people, like many of us. Most of them just don't hang around the resorts where we vacation.

The beach is certainly a happy place for me. I calculate that at the time of this writing, based on the average number of weeks I go to the beach each year versus the number of weeks I've been on planet earth, I have spent roughly 98 weeks at a beach and 3,100 weeks away from a beach. I would hate to think that the only times I have been happy in life are those 98 weeks at the coastline. The simple truth is that most of us don't spend any significant amount of time at what we would deem our "happy place." That is because most of the living, coming and going, and working in and out of our everyday lives is spent in the valleys and streets of the mundane between coastlines and mountaintops. Perhaps that's the point.

Jesus is better—always.

When Jesus said in John 10:10 (NKJV), "I have come that they may have life, and that they may have it more abundantly," His intent was not to move everyone to their favorite vacation spot or beyond their bleak circumstances. The word "abundantly" in this verse means *much more* or *greater.* In other words, Jesus is better—always.

Of course, we feel God's presence much more vividly across the ocean tide and ranging mountaintops. But He's just as present and vivid in the hospital room or the lonely street corner. The "happy place" is not some magical, geographic location or mythical state of mind. It's a person. His name is Jesus.

Because of this truth, it means the "happy place" can be found in the hospital room, the isolated nursing home, the grinding workplace, the dark back alley, the pavement of our driveways, the steps to our front door, the delightful dinner table, and so many more places. Every routine moment can be stupendously spectacular! These moments and places surround us every single day. The key is stepping out of the dullness of the ordinary to see and hear them. They do not rest on the surface. They require perspective and faith—the supernatural. Who gives you that? Only the Person, the Savior, the Spirit, and the Lord: Jesus.

Once you discover this transcendental truth, you'll never have to get in a car or on a plane just to find your "happy place." It will show up at your doorstep daily, and when it does, you'll gladly pull out a chair, give it a place to sit, and take in the impeccable setting all around you.

The "happy place" is not some magical, geographic location or mythical state of mind. It's a person. His name is Jesus.

34

Daily Rhythms & Loudness

There is a moment of discontinuity each day of my life that takes place in my driveway. It has been this way for the last twenty years. This moment occurs in my car. This moment is the space in between when I pull into my driveway after a long, compressed day of work and before I get out of the car to be home with my family. Some days, this moment happens while the sun is still up. Other days, it happens long after the sun has retired for the day and the moon is running its night shift.

In this moment, I make every attempt to leave behind the events that occurred in my day—good or bad—and turn my focus, and the little bit of energy I have left, onto my family. Some days, my endeavor is met with success. Other days, not so much, but it is not for lack of effort or intent. This is the one moment of my day where everything falls silent, and I take a breath. I prepare to trade one set of noise for another. No matter how loud the turbulence of my day has been, it will not compare to the loudness on the other side of the front door of my house. It will just be a different sort of noise and commotion.

In this fleeting moment of discontinuity and stillness, I come to the realization that in the moments behind me, I've had the opportunity to work, contribute, and be one small part of the grand narrative of life that God uses to write and form each day and turn it toward the grand end when Jesus returns. I will be tempted to think the work day was just another day of punching the clock to grind out a living. I will be tempted to think the moments I've experienced and the people I've crossed paths with are just random. But nothing could be further from the truth.

There are seemingly random moments like this in the Scriptures. One can read through lists of genealogies in books like Genesis and feel like you've been cast into a sea of boredom. What do unfamiliar, unpronounceable names like Arphaxad, Shem, Eber, and Peleg have to do with anything in my life today, or the big picture for that matter? One need only to read on to discover that through history, they all lead to a man named Jesus, who would ultimately save and change the world. In Scripture and in life, the smaller parts, the supposedly unattractive details, always lead to the grandness of God's mission.

> The daily rhythms of my life are part of the greater cadence of God's tempo, all pointing to the grand finale.

As a result, big or small, good or bad, whether I've messed it up or done it right, if I live my life unto the One who has fashioned and formed my being, every part of my day matters, and every part is pointing to something. That is worth waking up for, and that is worth carrying on until my task on earth is done.

As mundane or undesirable as they may seem, the daily rhythms of my life are part of the greater cadence of God's tempo, all pointing to the grand finale. I trust this by faith, even when my circumstances seem like they're saying something different. This gives every moment extreme value and marvelous possibilities!

I pause, take a breath, and prepare myself for what lies on the other side of the front door of my house. If the moments I have already encountered so far in my daily rhythm have such grand potential, then consider the wonder of possibilities lying before me with the ones who share my blood and DNA! There will be bikes to ride, games to play, homework to complete, events to discuss, balls to throw, meals to prepare, practices and games to attend, and perhaps even simple moments to sit on the couch and watch our favorite show or movie together. There will also be household chores, bills to pay, pets to feed, and maybe a few other undesirable tasks that make up the rhythms of our lives. Every enterprise behind the front door will wring out every ounce of remaining stamina I have left in me. Then we all lay our heads down at night, only to rise a few hours later and repeat the same rhythm all over again.

> True joy is being totally aware of how much grandness and promise exist in the routine of day-to-day living.

Though it's not required, if we're fortunate enough, we may have a few pinnacle moments along the way. Perhaps a trip to the coast, a getaway to a mountain peak, an excursion to an amusement park or exotic location, any of which could provide us needed rest and lasting memories. Thankfully, life finds its rhythms in the highest of peaks and lowest of valleys. I have experienced them all. But I have discovered that most of the living in this life is done in the mundane moments of daily rhythms and routines. True joy will never be found in the pinnacles alone. True joy will never be found in waiting for the next thing or the next highlight to come along. True joy is being totally aware of how much grandness and promise exist in the routine of day-to-day living.

There's a moment in the Bible when God made a promise to a childless and heirless Abraham. The promise was that his descendants would be so many, they would be like the "sand on the seashore" (Gen. 32:12). If it were me, I would tend to think the babies would start pouring out of my wife at this point. "Okay, God, the pinnacle can start happening any moment now!" But nothing happened for years after that promise. Both Abraham and his wife grew into old age and were well past childbearing age.

Imagine Abraham sitting at the interchange between what God has promised and the reality of his actual circumstances. Life seemed to just continue to be filled with ordinary moments of randomness. But nothing could be further from the truth. Romans 4:18 (NLT) tells us that in this in-between space, Abraham kept hoping, even when there was no reason for hope. At the ripe old age of 100, when his wife's womb was practically dead, they gave birth to a son. A pinnacle moment, of course. But according to Romans 4:19-20 (NLT), every mundane moment up until that point had been a pinnacle moment because he refused to stop believing that every mundane moment mattered and was pointing to something. As a result, his faith grew.

> There is a great moment when you find the grandness in your circumstances, even when they haven't turned or changed at your desired pace.

Like Abraham, you may be sitting in a moment of discontinuity and interchange between what you hoped for and the reality of your circumstances. If you focus simply on your circumstances, you will be left overwhelmed by what you deem to be random and pointless. But if, like Abraham, you focus on the God controlling your circumstances, you will find your faith strengthened beyond description, and you will experience the wonder of being able to find the miracle in the mundane. There is a great moment when you find the grandness in your circumstances, even when they haven't turned or changed at your desired pace.

So, I close my eyes, take a breath, pull a smile across my face, and feel exuberant joy shoot through my weary veins. The moments ahead, just behind that front door, will require everything of me, but I'm excited for the possibilities and future memories they hold! They hold the potential to lift life above the ordinary—right there in the routine! They will be loud and boisterous, and I may be tempted to desire an exit. But I will not entertain even the hint of such a thought. For I know that one day soon, these loud moments will be a distant memory. The silence I thought I wanted will be deafening, and I will long to have them back again. I open the door, lift up my head, and embrace the here and now for all that it wonderfully offers me. Thank you, Lord.

35

I Was Raised This Way

I was raised this way...I was a freshman in college and a scholarship athlete, and it was the first weekend our coach had required us to stay on campus for the weekend to train and practice. Sunday morning rolled around, and I was confronted with one of my first significant decisions as an independent adult. My body woke itself up early that Sunday morning, just as it had been doing every Sunday morning for all of my life up until that point.

At that time in history, unlike today, Sunday morning had a little bit of reverence regarding church and worship. Stores were closed, and no team practices or sporting events were scheduled. We had the morning free. I rolled out of my bed, and as my feet hit the ground, the first thought that popped in my head was, *Am I going to go worship in a church today?* I had been brought up in one church my entire life. I had been raised to believe that if you were in town, it was important to be in church. Honestly, until I left for college, the decision was generally made for me. I would be in church, end of story. I was raised that way.

> The Church still matters, and you're still part of it.

But all of a sudden, for the first time in my life, it was my decision

235

and my decision alone to make. No one else was around to influence, encourage, or convince me to go. For the first time in my life, I felt like I had the freedom to make the choice. Ah, sweet freedom! It would be so easy to roll back over in my bed. I was tired from the weekend's workouts. Besides, college students like me don't go to church...right?

I ducked my head back under the covers. *No one will know, and I could get used to this,* I told myself. As soon as my head hit the pillow, a voice subtly rang in my head in response to my thought, "But Jesus will know, and He won't let you get used to it. The Church still matters, and you're still part of it, college student or not."

When you come to faith in Jesus, He imparts His Holy Spirit on the inside of you to comfort, convict, guide, and lead you into the truth of your relationship with God. I'm so thankful the Lord spoke up that

> Now the Lord is the Spirit, and where the Spirit of the Lord is, there is freedom.
>
> 2 CORINTHIANS 3:17

day. No, the voice was not audible, but it clearly engaged my spirit, mind, and heart. As much as I wanted the voice to go away and for God's Spirit to stop talking, He would not.

I sat back up and told myself, *Well, I can't get in my car and leave campus, and there's only one church on campus. So, I guess I'll be attending Wingate Baptist Church today.* And that's what I did that Sunday morning. I was raised that way. I made a choice to go worship with church folk.

As I sat in the pew that morning, I thought to myself, *Isn't the true mark of coming into adulthood supposed to be measured by how many wild parties you attend, how much beer you drink, or how many sexual escapades you can have? Wasn't that supposed to mark my coming of age and newfound freedom to make decisions on my own? Congratulations, Carnes, you marked yours by putting on khaki pants and going to church! How lame.*

Even though I thought it, strangely, I didn't feel that way in my heart. I actually felt as free as I had ever been. As I walked back to my campus dorm that day after the worship service, that sense of freedom continued to overwhelm me and make my heart smile. For the first time, I understood 2 Corinthians 3:17 (ESV), "Now the Lord is the Spirit, and where the Spirit of the Lord is, there is freedom."

True freedom is having the choice between right and wrong and choosing what is right in spite of what you'd prefer to do, even if it costs you something. But sometimes, true freedom may have little to do with what is right and what is wrong. Sometimes it may be as simple as choosing between what benefits you most and what benefits those around you most. True freedom is when you make a decision that doesn't put you in the king's chair or put your preferences out in front. True freedom is when you choose to serve others rather than yourself. I was raised that way.

> True freedom is when you choose to serve others rather than yourself.

Did I choose to go to church out of guilt that day? Absolutely not. That would have been the wrong reason to go. Did I choose to go to church out of obligation? In part, yes, and that has value. I do a lot of things in my life out of obligation, and it's made me and the people around me better.

Did I choose to go to church out of duty and sacrifice? In part, yes, and that has value. Duty and sacrifice have always made me better when I apply them to my life. Nations are built on such noble traits.

But honestly, I chose to go to church that day because of love. I love Jesus because He loved me first, rescued me, and changed my life. I love God's people, and I love to worship with them in spite of imperfections. I love the church and its mission. I believe that I'm called to that mission, and I believe that it's the greatest mission on earth. It was

Sunday morning, I was in town, and I was in church, worshiping with other believers. I was raised this way.

For a moment, the thought entered my head, *Wasn't I supposed to rebel against this type of thinking at this stage of my life? Wasn't I supposed to make some type of public pronouncement against the church? Wasn't I supposed to deconstruct my faith or at least question it? Did I miss something?* No, actually a thousand little weekly choices my parents made each Sunday morning, in getting us up and taking us to church to worship and thank God with other believers over the first 18 years of my life, led to this one significant choice I made on my own. This was the day when I drew a line in the sand for the Church on my own, and I haven't been the same since.

> I chose to go to church that day because of love. Hundreds of little choices on routine days gave me the ability to make the right choice when I needed it most.

Accountability pushed me that day. Duty and sacrifice raised my expectations that day. But above all else, love compelled me that day, and I was as free as I'd ever been. I was raised that way.

As I look across the landscape of Sunday mornings these days, I'm not sure many are raised this way anymore. For those who are: stay the course and persevere. It's worth it. Every battle, every choice, and every stand matters. They did for me. Hundreds of little choices on routine days gave me the ability to make the right choice when I needed it most. That was the day my faith became my own. Not because I broke away from something, but because I affirmed something I knew was right when I had the choice to do the opposite. I was raised this way, and I couldn't feel more free!

36

The Miracle of A Changed Life

It was my junior year of college. I stood on a couch in the middle of a dorm room, Bible in hand, preaching to a bunch of drunk college students. I was not a partyer or a drinker in college, but I was a friend to many who did party and binge drink. I went to many parties with them. I was their designated driver. I got a lot of free meals that way. I had no problem mixing it up and having fun with the best partyers. I just did it sober. I didn't begrudge them their fun. I just tried to be a witness by showing them they could have as much fun without it.

I made that choice mostly because of my personal Christian convictions but also because my dad was an alcoholic, as were many in my family history. I was living through that trauma, and I was always aware of where my choices could land me.

Nonetheless, these were my friends. They loved and respected me, and I respected and loved them. This is probably the only reason they gave me the platform they gave me that night. Typically, if you tried preaching to a group of drunk college students, you'd get thrown out the window on your rear end. But something worse happened to me that night.

Let me be clear: love for them or Jesus didn't motivate my preaching that night. I'm sure that in some twisted way, being that my dad was still an alcoholic, I was preaching to my dad and myself. I was likely wailing against them for the hurt that was happening in my life.

Then, as I reached the crescendo of my sermon, one of my childhood friends, with whom I went to the same church and who knew my family well, yelled back at me, "Your own daddy drinks as much or more than anybody in town!" Of course, I was already aware of this. I just didn't know anyone else knew. I did my best to hide it from people. Now, everyone in the room knew it. The self-righteous preacher was the son of an alcoholic. It pierced through me like a knife. I stepped off the couch. The sermon was over. The room fell silent. There was nothing left to say. As I walked back to my room, heartbroken, I muttered to myself, "They'll never change."

Over twenty years later, I had an encounter with that same childhood friend who yelled at me about my dad that fateful night. Unknown to me, after graduation from college, he had spent many years battling alcoholism himself. He almost lost his life because of it. When we saw each other again, the first thing he said to me was, "I'm sorry for what I said to you that night about your dad. I know I hurt you." The reality confronted me that, up until that moment, I did not remember that night for over twenty years. My brain had likely suppressed it due to the trauma.

Fast-forward to January of 2021, when I heard him give the eulogy at his brother's funeral. I knew I had to reach out to him. We arranged to meet for dinner. When we sat down, my first question to him was, "Why did you apologize to me, and how did you remember that night?" Being sober for five years, he spoke of how part of the 12-step program was to apologize to the people you hurt. But more than that, with tears in his eyes, he said he knew that he hurt me. I never knew he felt that way.

He went on to tell me that after battling alcohol addiction for much of his adult life, he had decided that he could not stop drinking and was beyond hope. So, he got in his car and started driving. He decided he would drink until he either died or passed out and had a car crash. He passed out and, by the grace of God, his car came to a slow halt in the middle of the highway at 4:00 a.m. As he sat there, a stranger appeared out of nowhere and pulled him to the side of the road. The stranger looked at him and told him help was on the way and that he would pray for him. That night, after blowing into the breathalyzer, my friend's blood alcohol content was beyond the lethal dose anyone should have in their body. He should have been dead. He was not. He never saw that "stranger" again. He's been sober since. Divine intervention.

As we spoke, I was amazed. This was not the same person I knew all those years, and most certainly not the one I drove around while he was drunk so many times. He pointed to God and Jesus being the only reason he was still alive.

I prayed for my dad for close to twenty years to get sober, but there were times I lost hope. He finally did get sober, and our relationship has never been closer. I walked away from my friend that night in a college dorm, thinking he'd never change. Yet, here we sat, twenty-nine years later, with me amazed at how much God had changed him.

God has never ceased to astound me with how much He can change a life with His amazing grace. That night in that drunken dorm room, I exhorted a group of drunk friends to try and sing the hymn "Amazing Grace." I was convinced that my childhood friend, with whom I grew up singing that hymn in church, would not have the conviction to sing it while drunk. But he rose and sang it to the top of his lungs with the rest of them that night. I was amazed.

But I was even more amazed when that same friend sat across from me and spoke of the amazing grace of God that had kept him, saved him, and never let go of him all those years. I would have never thought it possible, but God can change anyone.

No matter who you are, what you've done, where you've been, or how long you've done it, God can do a work in you. It doesn't matter how hopeless your situation may be; God can change anyone. I've seen that miracle with my own eyes. No one is beyond hope—no one.

> God can change anyone. No one is beyond hope—no one.

Of course, it's still hard, and it's still a fight, but God redeemed my friend's brokenness after all those years. He redeemed mine also. We were both changed and awash in God's grace. Maybe it was time for another verse of "Amazing Grace."

37

Was It Worth It?

"You should be able to go at least fifty miles on these. This charge should easily get you all over the island with the time span you're going to have these bikes."

Those were the words spoken by one of the store managers who dropped off the set of electric bikes where my family and I were staying in Oak Island, NC. We were renting the bikes for an afternoon of fun and adventure. We were on vacation for my oldest son Jadon's graduation trip from high school. My wife had not joined us yet. My youngest son, Baylon, was not old enough to drive a bike by himself, so, much to his dismay, he would have to ride on the back of one of the bikes with me. Off we went, Baylon and I rode on one bike, and my other two sons, Jadon and Ryder, rode bikes by themselves.

We peddled and throttled all the way up to one end of the island, reaching speeds of 20 mph as we rode. Wind in our faces, gleefully laughing and smiling, we rode in the hot beach sun as far as we could go. We were having the time of our lives. Once we reached the end of the beach, we decided to turn around and go back to the other end of the island, which was a former Civil War Fort called Fort Caswell.

Once again, with the warm sun on our shoulders and the wind whisking across our faces, we were off. Smiles and laughter abounded as we rode the long miles down along the coastline to the destination that once served as a military garrison for the entire island. Though I had done it many times before by myself, I had planned to take my boys and explore the old tunnels of the broken-down fortress. It would have been a first for them. Then, out of nowhere... mission aborted.

Just as we approached the gates of the Fort, the batteries on two of the bikes sputtered and died. We were miles from the house where we were staying with friends. You can peddle electric bikes, but they are not made for peddling, at least not the ones we were riding. The electric bikes we were riding weighed about eighty pounds. A typical road bicycle weighs about 18 pounds. I ride a road bike often for exercise. These electric bikes were not exactly material for peddling down the road with ease in the hot summer sun. Nonetheless, there we were.

Fittingly, my oldest son Jadon's bike still had its charge. It was his graduation trip, so I suppose it's only fair. Office hours for the rental place had ended. All we had was a pick-up time back at the house, approximately 45 minutes from the time the batteries went out and three hours past the time we had received the bikes. *Not too bad,* I thought. *But still not what the guy promised us. It is what it is. This is the situation. We have miles to peddle and a lot of work to do.*

We decided to stick Baylon on the bike with Jadon, since his bike still had charge. Ryder and I would peddle back and meet them at the house. Jokingly, I told Jadon, "If we're not back in an hour, send the rescue crew out for us, or just send a truck to pick up the remains." Not wanting to leave us, Jadon put Baylon on the back of his bike and rode alongside us most of the way back.

We began to peddle 80 pounds of metal and aluminum, plus our body weight, without battery assist, in the hot summer sun, the miles and miles back to the house. You could not adjust the seats on these bikes for leverage. They sat low, so you got little leverage unless you stood up. There were minimal gear changes on the bike. Onward, trudging and laboring, we went. There was no more wind in our faces, just the hot sun on our backs. The laughter turned to measured breathing for the long road ahead.

> I wondered what I had missed in trying to get out of those less-than-ideal moments of my life.

About midway back, my middle son Ryder, sweat dripping down his brow, turned to me and asked, "Dad, since the bikes lost charge and we're having to peddle back, do you think it was worth it?" I paused and thought, then wiped the sweat from my bald forehead. Continuing to pedal with force, I turned to him and said with utmost certainty, "Absolutely!" I made sure to say it loud enough so that my other two sons could hear as well.

I continued, "Look around, son. The coastline is on your left, your brothers are on your right, and I'm here beside you. It doesn't matter the situation we're facing; we are all together, and I wouldn't trade anything for that. I'd do it all over again to get this moment right here." There was no response from any of my boys—only silence. It was a weighty, impactful moment in a set of less-than-ideal circumstances.

The rest of the ride, we talked about things we hadn't talked about since they were little kids. Their faces weren't in their phones. All we had was each other, the moment, and the task at hand. We were creating a memory we would talk about for years, and I was immediately aware of it and glad, even as hard as it was. I sat back on the bike, continued to peddle, and rode along, taking every moment with me.

Then, I thought about all the less-than-ideal circumstances in life that I tried to hurry through or escape. I wondered what I had missed in trying to get out of those less-than-ideal moments of my life. How much better would I be if I had noticed my surroundings, kept peddling, and rode along rather than resisting?

In all that labor of peddling and less-than-ideal, I discovered I had more than I could ever ask for. I discovered that no matter how bad less-than-ideal becomes, the weight of the good around me has always outweighed the bad. The experience I was getting with those who labored with me vastly outweighed the labor of peddling 80 pounds of metal.

God's faithfulness is always like that as long as I take the time to look beyond my circumstances. There's value in the suffering, value in the labor, value in the work, value in the grieving, and value in every less-than-ideal circumstance. We may not feel it as we ride through it, but we can always look back and say, "Yeah, it was absolutely worth it." This is why we "fix our eyes not on what is seen, but on what is unseen, since what is seen is temporary, but what is unseen is eternal" 2 Corinthians 4:18 (NIV).

There's value in every less-than-ideal circumstance.

We crested the hill and began to coast the last half-mile to the house. As we did, the guy from the rental company met us in his truck to pick up the bikes. We had just made it in time. He parked the truck and, as he exited the vehicle, looked up and asked excitedly, "Well, how'd it go? Did you all have a good time? Aren't those bikes easy and worth it?"

I paused, and then I told him about the batteries going dead. He apologized and offered a discount for the next ride. I looked around at my boys and thought about the last hour of hard peddling and the moments we shared, and then responded simply, "No doubt, we had a ton of fun as

> The moment everything got hard, that's when it became worth it.

we coasted down the coastline under the ease the batteries gave us. However, though I never would have thought it, the moment the batteries died and everything got hard, we all pressed in to ride and work together; that's when it became worth it." Strangely and fittingly, it generally works the same way in life.

38

Running To The School Bus

As a sixteen-year-old high school student, one of the things I loved most about getting my driver's license was the fact that I would no longer have to ride the bus to school. I was reluctant to ride the school bus because I was in two different wrecks while riding it. I threw a rock and accidentally busted out a window of a school bus. Half the fights I ever got into in my life were on a school bus. I was bullied on a school bus. I heard language on a school bus that I heard nowhere else. I saw things on a school bus I saw nowhere else. I learned more about what *not* to do in life while riding a school bus than what *to* do in life.

Over the course of my early years in school, I went from being scared to ride the school bus, to tolerating the school bus, to being embarrassed to ride the school bus, to hating to ride the school bus. I suppose it's safe to say while it did toughen me up quite a bit, the school bus held little in the way of affirmation in my life.

If you live long enough, trouble will find you.

That is why I wrestled greatly over whether to let my kids ride the bus to school when they were small children. Eventually, convenience won out, and my kids rode the bus like I did. However, unlike me, they wanted to ride the bus, which is another reason we let them. As much as I was able, I tried to see my boys off to school and watch them get on the bus each morning. The routine was always the same: gather to pray, watch them walk to the end of the street, wave, smile, shout, and then watch them ride off.

But the fifth-grade year of my youngest son, Baylon, was quite different than any other year. It happened on the first day of school and continued every day to the last day of school in 2020. He did something I didn't expect., something I never would have done in all my years of riding the bus to school. He ran to the school bus stop. Down the street, to the corner, he would go. Backpack shaking rigorously on his back, he would sprint. He made that run every day of the school year. I fell in love with it from the moment I first saw it. He was never

> As Goliath moved closer to attack, David quickly ran out to meet him.
>
> 1 SAMUEL 17:48

late for the bus. He ran by choice, of his own free will, with such passion, excitement, and enthusiasm. No one made him do it; he chose it.

The first time I saw him do it, I admired his passion, enthusiasm, and vigor. I loved the posture he chose. His bus was yellow like mine. His bus was slow like mine. He heard profanity and was ridiculed on his bus like me. His bus was big and loud like mine. He dealt with people who picked on him like I did. But he ran to his bus. I labored to get the courage and strength to walk to my bus. I scorned the proposition of getting on my bus. Baylon went like lightning to his bus—*every single day.*

The more I watched him run that school year, the more I thought to myself, *I wonder if certain things in my life would have been different if I had taken the posture to run to the bus?* I spent a good bit of my high school years and the first two years of college running from things I should have run toward. But at about age 20, something clicked in me, and I began running toward things rather than running away from them. As a result, I've spent my adult life running toward less-traveled roads. Probably for good and bad. I often wonder if any of that is some subconscious reaction to running from things in my first twenty years.

In life you don't get to choose what or who is on your bus. You don't get to cushion the events of your life; you don't get to manipulate or steer away from all trouble or hardship. If you live long enough, trouble will find you. You can try to avoid it, and you may be successful temporarily, but I'm not convinced you'll be better for avoiding hardship. You won't always be able to steer around the "bus stops" of life. But you can choose how you go toward or through them.

> When Joseph went in to do his work, she came and grabbed him by his cloak, demanding, 'Come and sleep with me!' Joseph tore himself away, leaving his cloak in her hand, as he ran from the house.
>
> GENESIS 39:11-12

Recording the famed story of the battle between David and Goliath in the Bible, 1 Samuel 17:48 (NLT) says, "As Goliath moved closer to attack, David quickly ran out to meet him." I've always loved that verse. David wasn't positioning himself or looking for trouble, nor should we. However, when trouble came looking for him, he ran toward the battle.

Of course, there are also battles we need to have sense enough to run away from. In Genesis 39:11-12 (NLT), a man named Joseph ran from his master's wife when she tried to seduce him to go to bed with her. "One day, when no one else was around, when Joseph went in to do his work, she came and grabbed him by his cloak, demanding, 'Come and sleep with me!' Joseph tore himself away, leaving his cloak in her hand, as he ran from the house." His character and commitment to God enabled Joseph to make the right choice.

In life there will be times when we need to have enough sense and humility to run from certain battles. There is no shame or cowardice in that, only the character of God. It could even be argued that it takes more courage to know when to run from a battle than to run toward one. That said, there will also be times in life when the battle begins to advance toward us, and the time for retreating is over. In those moments, we'll also need the courage and the strength of God to run toward the battle and fight. Only staying on our knees in prayer before God can provide us the wisdom to know the difference between the two.

> I want to be able to get up each day and run toward the events of that day with hope, expectancy, and passion—no matter what I may be facing.

Many days, Baylon got off the bus with a rough story. Some of those stories included running toward battles, and others included being wise enough to run away. But he always got up and ran to the bus stop with enthusiasm the next day. I want to be able to get up each day and run toward the events of that day with hope, expectancy, and passion—no matter what I may be facing. If I get knocked down, if I fail, so be it. God grant me the strength to get up and run back the next day!

I don't want to cower in fear. I don't want anxiety or worry to paralyze me. I want to be able to run toward my dreams and not away from them. I want to run toward every breath I'm given! Even if I'm unsure about what I'm running toward may hold, I want to take delight in that momentary dash! If the backpack I'm carrying is heavy and shakes rigorously behind me with the weight from the stress of life, let it never stop me! Even if I face great trepidation, I want to run like a kid running to the school bus stop. And if I look back, I want to see my Heavenly Father standing in the road smiling in approval, shouting, and basking in the joy of the run with me.

39

The Perfect, Out of Place, Pace

It was the fall of 2004 in Roanoke, VA. My wife and I made the trip up to visit her parents for the weekend. There was the usual distinct chill in the air, the kind that would leap across your skin, shoot through your lungs as you breathed it in, and make you come alive. The leaves were colored and washed in the glow of vivid red, gold, and bright orange, each colored by the brush of God, to give us a sense of awe, wonder, and gratitude. The slight breeze that blew through the leaves seemed to be the whistle of God as He carefully and intently loosened the leaves from the trees to fall gently to the ground, acquainting us with the reality that He is always preparing to make all things new.

It was the perfect day for a run. So, I laced up my shoes and went down the streets. This day, my route would take me through a local park. As usual, the day would be filled with activity, and I was moving from event to event. My run was sandwiched between scheduled events. I didn't need to tarry, and I had to be purposed. Time, as always, was of the essence.

Strangely, so much of my life then and now seems to match the hurriedness of that run. Yes, I was aware of and enjoying the beauty of that fall day, but I was also enslaved to the pace of the world around me. That is when the gift rounded the corner of the greenway and stared me straight in the face.

He was a tall elderly man, 88 years old, to be exact. He was dressed in brown khaki pants, a tan shirt, and a dark brown sweater. He had a matching brown fedora on his head. He walked with a cane, slightly bent over at the back. As we almost collided, our eyes locked, and I blurted out, "Dr. Gamble!?"

His head cocked, he bore the grandest smile, and he replied, "Why, Mark Carnes, how are you doing? Come, let's sit on this bench and talk awhile."

Dr. Harry Gamble was my wife's pastor as a child, where she grew up at Calvary Baptist Church. He had been retired several years, but he still knew her family well. More than that, he knew my family well. We shared Waxhaw, NC as our hometown. Of course, his history went back much further than mine. He was born there in 1916.

> I was enslaved to the pace of the world around me.

Dr. Gamble and I were well-acquainted on many levels. We also shared a calling and life's work in full-time ministry. But when he said, "Let's sit on this bench and talk awhile," my first thought was, *Uh, I don't have a while. I'm on a bit of a schedule.* But, of course, where do you think I ended up? That is correct: sitting on that bench. But more than the beauty of a brisk, fall day, that encounter was God's gift to me.

Dr. Gamble began to ask me about my family, my wife's family, my job in ministry, and many other things. He took a keen interest in some of the most mundane details as if they were of utmost importance. He began each sentence by putting his hand on my shoulder, leaning in, and saying, "Now, Maaaaark." He said my name like it was a great pleasure for him. My name is one syllable, but he made it two.

His speech was deep and thundering, yet thoughtful and kind. He spoke with a deliberate and focused pace, absorbing each word before releasing it into the atmosphere. It was genuine. He captured my attention right there in that park. He made me feel like I was the only person on earth.

When he began to speak of Waxhaw, a glow came across his face that seemed to radiate with child-like excitement. He spoke of the old days and times gone by. Then, he spoke of the bridge in Waxhaw that spans over the railroad tracks, running through the middle of town. He declared that one hasn't truly lived until they stand at the center of that bridge, close their eyes, and breathe in the rich and resplendent Waxhaw air! I've done that. He's right.

He refused to be hurried or worried.

But what struck me most was his pace about everything. It was so different than the hurried world around him. He gave attention and measured patience to everything. People were rushing to and fro all about him, and yet his pace was so different and out of place. It was perfect. He wasn't unaware of the events around him, but they didn't control him. He refused to be hurried or worried.

He knew of the bad. He prayed over it. But he knew there was always good in the midst of the bad, and that there was always far more good than bad in the eternal scheme of things. His peace, assurance, comfort, and pace came from something different than the world had to offer. The heaven that held that peace was in his heart, but he also knew he'd be going there soon. I wanted his pace, so out of place, so perfect. He wasn't out of touch; he knew what mattered most, and that is where he put most of his attention.

Finally, he said, "Well, I've taken up enough of your time," and got up to continue his walk. Strangely, all I wanted was to avoid that long talk, but now I didn't want it to end. As we parted, I looked at my watch—ouch! Over forty-five minutes had gone by, and the clock was still clicking. I had to move! I began to run.

Only a few steps into it, I thought back to the conversation on the bench with Dr. Gamble. I could almost hear him saying, "Now, Maaaark." I stopped running as I crested the top of the hill. From the valley I could see the colored mountains all around me. It's strange all you can see when you're not marching to the world's pace. I walked the rest of the way back. I took it all in.

Only months later, Dr. Gamble would breathe his last breath and go home to heaven. I wonder if he knew that would be the last time he'd ever see me. If I had not stopped that day, I would have never received the gift of the "perfect, out of place, pace" from an old pastor and friend. God used him to give it to me that day.

Slow down, step out of the traffic, and take a moment to be still before God and listen.

Slow down, step out of the traffic, and take a moment to be still before God and listen. See and know that He is in control and able. Take time for what matters. Notice the beauty. Don't let the rush crowd it out. Hear the sounds beneath the sounds. Don't let the hurry drown it out. Be thankful in every moment. Look at people when you talk to them, listen to them, love them, and care for them. Take an interest in them, and make them feel like they are the most important person in the world. Don't run through moments; grab and experience them, even the ones you don't think you have time for. Each one could be your last. Not one second you're trying to salvage is guaranteed. Slow down and breathe in what's important, not the noise.

I heard a story from my father-in-law about a message Dr. Gamble preached at their church from Psalm 46:10a (NIV). He got up and read the verse with his deep, thunderous voice, "Be still and know that I am God." Then, he calmly sat down in the pulpit in stillness and silence for the next 10 minutes, leaving the congregation to sit, stunned into stillness and silence as well. He was still preaching that message to me on a park bench some 40 years later, just months before he died.

"Step out of the traffic! Take a long, loving look at me, your High God, above politics, above everything."

Psalm 46:10 (The Message)

40

We Were Beautiful Once

There were days when we would run from one end of the playground to the other, permeating the air with screams of merriment. Afternoon bike rides turned to dusk adventures as we rode to faraway places across distant lands, all while never leaving the confines of our own small town. We dusted our knees and faces with little-league baseball games and squeaked our shoes across hardwood basketball floors while throwing balls into baskets for another two points.

The once jovial existence of our childhood seemed to sprint into adulthood with the speed of a locomotive through the countryside. In the blink of an eye, we all grew up. We are burying the people who, outside of God, once provided the only source of security we knew—our moms, dads, teachers, coaches, and Sunday School teachers. These important people taught us to play ball, manage money, spell, drive, and so much more. One by one, we are gathering to bid them farewell until we are joyfully reunited in eternity. As we share our tears and hugs, I am reminded of the distinct reality that we've grown older.

> Heaven is telling me this world is not my eternal home.

There was a time when graduation celebrations and weddings seemed to be the main reasons for gathering. I am now entering the phase of life when funerals threaten to become the prominent reason for gathering. With each glancing moment of our congregating, another life is remembered and celebrated. Each transitory moment reminds of the quickening truth that we've grown older.

I still recall the day I drove all on my own down the street as a sixteen-year-old in a white Oldsmobile Delta 88. Now, instead of driving away for the first time with my driver's license, I am watching my own kids drive away for the first time with their driver's license. I still remember the day I drove away and left them at kindergarten for the first time. The passage of time is so abrupt that it still feels like a few weeks ago.

I remember the Saturday afternoon my father helped me detail the black Mercedes I drove to my first-ever high school prom. Now, I am detailing each moment of my oldest son's preparations for his first-ever prom. As we gather to take pictures, we are surrounded by other parents who, not long ago, gathered for prom pictures of their own. The passage of time has occurred so swiftly that I am reminded again: we've grown older.

> Each transitory moment reminds of the quickening truth that we've grown older.

We gaze at our teenagers and marvel at the display of their youth and beauty. Their once adorable, child-like faces are giving over to adult features. We barely recognize them standing there, all made up and dressed so nicely. For a moment, we forget we once changed their diapers and strolled them through amusement parks. It wasn't that long ago, but the passage of time has been so immediate that I'm again struck with the matter that we've grown older. Most of us parents are in the middle-age transition, where we hold tightly to the fleeting youth we have left and brace for the onset of senior adulthood that will come all too quickly, if we're blessed enough to get there. We've grown older, but we're not that old yet.

We're all standing in a group, taking pictures of our kids before they head off to the prom. I glance to the left and notice a grandmother and grandfather. They are standing in the back, distanced from the group. They have gathered to witness the phenomenon of youth and beauty on display. They peer through the circle, but they are left out. They are not intentionally left out of the circle, but they are pushed there by the attention given to youth and beauty. Reluctantly, they've grown used to being on the outside of the circle. They realize they've grown old, and this is where most of society leaves them: on the outside looking in while youth and beauty take center stage.

We were beautiful once, too. I keep my gaze fixed on them. They are smiling, pleasant, and dutifully obedient to the scene and their place in it. Their posture takes a back seat. They have no choice. But I sense their eyes and hearts are screaming something different. Sadly, no one is listening. What are they screaming through their silent and patient visage? To hear it, I have to take my attention off the youth and beauty at the center of the spotlight. I watch, and I listen. Their expressions reveal it all as they silently say, "We were beautiful once, too." Their silent expressions reveal the battle with their thoughts and feelings.

> *There was a time when we were the center of attention. It's true, it really is; we were young and beautiful once as well. There was a time when others gathered around us, rather than in front of us. There was a time when we were strong. We could move as swiftly as the rest of you. There was a time when we were*

out front. There was a time when no one had to wait on us. There was a time when no one blew their horns at us because we were driving too slowly in traffic. There was a time when we sat up front, rather than in the back nearest to the restrooms. There was a time when it didn't matter where we parked or what time we ate.

I remember when we used to dance. We could dance all night. The aches and pains didn't bother us so much then. We still like to dance; we really do. In our minds, we don't feel any older. I suppose we've just gotten used to the fact that our bodies don't always cooperate anymore. There was a time when doctor's visits were only for emergencies rather than daily maintenance. We had dreams at one time. The truth is, we still do. But no one asks about them anymore.

Our grandkids bring us such joy. Perhaps they're one of the few things that help us feel younger. Sometimes, we comically watch them imitate us. We remember a time when we used to act like we were old, and everyone would laugh. But that was way back when we were beautiful, before we became old.

Many offer us counterfeit, well-intentioned compliments that we're aging gracefully. But is there such a thing? We fight our aging with ferocity every single day. Of course, aging has its place and its own value, but it doesn't make it any easier. Is it true that my best moments are behind me, and I am simply relegated to nothing more than memories of what used to be?

Oh, you should have been there to see it! We were beautiful, strong, and young once. Before social media and before photographs were taken with phones to capture every moment, we were beautiful. We have a few aged photographs to show you if you'd like to see or hear about them. But no one seems interested anymore. I guess you would've had to have been there to believe it. We were beautiful once, too.

Immediately, I think of my parents. Once stalwart with robust certainty and strength, they tackled life with such force. Yet now, they move with a slowness I find myself all too unprepared to handle. For a moment, I am submerged with the lament that at my own pace, I can push them to the rear of the circle at times.

I am quickly jolted back to reality as the flash and click of the cameras ends, and the cluster of youth and beauty we call "our kids" begins to disperse. Youth and beauty are still prominently on display. I am aware I have reached the phase of life where I'm beginning to get pushed out of the circle.

We get lost in what the world defines as true beauty and value.

It is then I realize the fleeting nature of the focus on youth and beauty, the spotlight, and being the center of attention. Unwittingly, we long for it. Yet, when we get it, we find it has no lasting or eternal merit. It only leaves us longing for more of that which we cannot fill. We get lost in what the world defines as true beauty and value.

My parents always told me true beauty comes from something much deeper within the soul. It is not found in the luster of outward appearance or the robust strength of youth. It is only as I watch them move with a more measured pace that I see this most clearly.

The words of Scripture in 2 Corinthians 4:16-17 (ESV) rouses this awareness within my soul. "So we do not lose heart. Though our outer self is wasting away, our inner self is being renewed day by day. For this light momentary affliction is preparing for us an eternal weight of glory beyond all comparison."

For those who know Christ, the struggle with aging is actually not a loss of youth and beauty. It is the body's way of recognizing that our soul is growing restless and weary with this temporary, broken-down world, and it is longing for its true home in glory. Our soul is who we really are and our true nature. Our bodies are temporary shells that, through the process of aging, send off the signal that we were made for something greater—eternity. We were not created to be compatible with this world. It is temporary. Our souls are made for our Creator. Through the process of time, the soul will shed these broken bodies to reveal its true beauty in glory.

As I watch my parents get frighteningly slower, and as I watch my own body quicken the pace toward this phase of life, I need only be reminded that heaven is telling me this world is not my eternal home. True eternal beauty draws nearer as temporary beauty fades with each passing day.

The world screams, "You're growing older and losing your beauty!" but heaven screams, "No, you're actually growing younger and edging toward true beauty for eternity!" Without question, youth and worldly beauty are a gift from God, and they should be celebrated and used to their maximum potential. However, they are short-lived and a reminder of this impermanent world.

> So we do not lose heart. Though our outer self is wasting away, our inner self is being renewed day by day. For this light momentary affliction is preparing for us an eternal weight of glory beyond all comparison.
>
> 2 CORINTHIANS 4:16-17

I peer back over at the elderly couple pushed to the edge of the courtyard that day, yet confidently taking their place out of the spotlight. Their wrinkled, smiling faces reveal a beauty that the world can never come close to touching. They were beautiful once, but they have far surpassed that definition. Now, they're glorious, and they are closer to touching the reality of that glory. Perhaps someone should put them in the center and take a picture. It's one of the closest things we have to a picture of heaven.

41
The Long Jump

When I was a small boy, there was a time when I wanted to be the world's greatest long jumper. At least, that's what I told myself. The problem was there was only one week out of the year when I would practice the long jump. It was the week my family took a vacation to North Myrtle Beach, SC.

Though I dreamed of one day being an Olympic long jumper, I was actually only interested in doing the long jump that one week of the year. There was no other day or time the rest of the entire year that I even gave long jumping a thought. It only occupied my mind and time for one hour each of the seven days we were in North Myrtle Beach.

The scenario was the same each day. After a long morning playing in the ocean and a satisfying lunch in our beach-front hotel room, we would take a short rest inside. Late afternoon would come, and that is when I would begin to beg my dad to take me down to the beach for the long jump session. No one else would do—not my mom or sister, only my dad. My dad would grab his hat and a towel, and off we would go to the sand for an hour of long jumping.

In the soft, hot, white sands of North Myrtle Beach, my dad would slowly mark off a starting jump line. This would be the line from which I would take off and leap through the air, jumping as far as I could. The landing line would change each time, depending on the distance of my jump.

I would back up the proper number of paces from the jumping off line and wait for my dad to shout, "Go!" Then, I would make a mad dash for that line and jump as far as I could through the hot, salty air. While flying through the air, I would imagine an Olympic stadium filled with thousands of people gathered to see me set the world record. I would try to emulate the form of the world's greatest long jumpers. I would stretch out my feet as far as I could for the landing. As I landed, sand would fly everywhere around me. My dad would quickly come in and mark the spot where my feet landed. Then, he would carefully measure the distance of the jump.

Those moments were some of the few in my childhood I ever had alone with my dad.

Each time, I would go back and try to break the previous distance, again and again, until I was too tired to do it anymore. Any time I would jump past the previous jump, my dad would give me the measurement, and I would leap in the air and give him a high five. I would shout and smile. He would shout and smile. I would then joyously ask him, "Do you think that jump was good enough, Dad!? Do you think I'll make it to the Olympics one day!?" We would then discuss the hopeful possibilities and dream together.

For one hour, it was just me and my dad. No one else. It didn't matter how many other people were on the beach. For that hour, it was if we were the only ones there. We laughed, played, high-fived, dreamed, talked, finished, and walked back—together. Me and my dad.

Years went by, and I outgrew the long jump and exchanged that dream for a few others. As I reflected on those moments when it was my dad and I on the beach, I came to the stark realization that those moments were some of the few in my childhood I ever had alone with him. Those moments were just a few where I ever had his full attention, devoted purely and solely to me. Those days at the beach were some of the few when he didn't have something else in life competing for his attention.

It wasn't that my dad didn't love me, care for me, or want to spend time with me. It's just that back home, there was always work, always something that needed to be done, and always other important things competing for his time and attention. He was the sole financial provider for our family, as my mom stayed home with my sister and I. That was a decision they made together.

> What I was really begging for was time with my dad. Everything else was secondary.

Being in upper management of the banking industry and an upstanding and participating member of our local church and the town in which we lived put tremendous pressure on my dad from all sides. Being a father and a husband and providing for the needs of your family are some of life's most difficult tasks. Giving everything its proper time allotment seems almost impossible. I have discovered this to be true in my own life.

When I think about those late afternoons at the beach, the long jump was never really about the long jump. The dreams were never really about the Olympics. The distance of the jumps never really mattered. What I was really begging for was time with my dad. Everything else was secondary.

The leaping in the air only meant something because my dad was watching. The take-off, the landing, and the distance only mattered because my dad was coming in quickly to measure and high-five when it was done. Out of the thousands of people I imagined watching from an Olympic stadium, only one of them mattered: my dad. His gaze was fixed on me, and that was all I wanted. The hour only mattered because, for that time period, it was the two of us and no one else. We laughed, high-fived, smiled, and played—together. That was actually the dream.

A child needs their parents. There are things that only a mother can do, and there are things only a father can do. A child needs them both, together, in the home and creating a stable environment. Sadly, too few children seem to get that these days. A father needs to come home after work. He needs to be engaged, no matter how tired he may be after a long day's work. The effort is worth it.

In the movie, *Avengers: End Game,* Tony Stark famously said, "No amount of money ever bought a second of time." It is true. Take the time.

My dad was no different than many dads in his generation or mine. He worked hard, came home each night, honored his word and commitments, honored his marriage vows, and provided for his family. He struggled with not being able to do everything or be at every event. I have the same struggle with my own boys. My dad was a great dad despite his imperfections. He made many things possible for me and my own children because he worked so hard and thought about our future. I wouldn't be where I am today without his sacrifice for our family.

But also like many, there were times we missed together. There were more things I would have loved to do together. I don't begrudge my dad for those things. It simply happened. Holding bitterness or an unforgiving spirit does no one any good. It only cripples what lies ahead.

I am thankful that later in life, my dad and I have made up for a lot of those lost times. He was able to give more of himself away as he progressed through the different stages of aging and life. There have been many sweet moments in my adult life that we have experienced together, and I am thankful for all of it. It doesn't matter how old you grow, you always need your dad and desire time with him. That desire never dies or ages out.

Maybe you're a dad or mom who has struggled to be the parent you wanted to be and feel like you constantly came up short. If you've made your share of mistakes or your own parents made their share of mistakes, you cannot change the past. What is done is done.

But you do have the great opportunity to own what you can, make a sincere and loving apology, extend forgiveness, and move forward, no longer bound by bitterness and anguish. It's never too late to start somewhere. It will take incredible humility, selflessness, and courage, but it is a far better option than choosing to continually drift along the sea of regret and bitterness.

> A child needs their parents. It doesn't matter how old you grow, you always need your dad and desire time with him.

To this day, each time I walk across the hot, white sands of Myrtle Beach, I think about those late afternoon long jumping sessions from my childhood with my dad. Just a young kid and his dad spending time together. The simplicity of those moments helped define the man I am today. Those moments remind me to turn off the computer, put down the phone, show up even when it gets hard, and give all my effort to my own wife and children. No dream, gold medal, or Olympic stadium will ever duplicate the wonder of a family pouring their love into each other.

Today, in the sifting of the hot sand between my toes as I walk across it many years later, I can feel the brush of my dad's hand across mine in a high five. I can see him kneeling down to measure the distance of the jump. I can still see his smile. But most of all, in the warmth of the ocean breeze, I can still hear him saying in the best way he knew how, "I love you. You matter." It didn't always have to come with words; it came with seconds, minutes, and hours—*time.* No amount of money could ever pay for that.

42
Seashells

One of my favorite things to do is run on the beach. On one particular vacation, I decided to rise early and run with the sunrise. While running, I looked down to see a small fragment of what I believed to be a conch shell sticking out of the sand. There wasn't much of the shell protruding through the thick, dark sand, but it was enough to stop me in my tracks. As I stooped over to try and pick it up, I wondered, *What if, just what if, this shell is still intact?* If it was, it would be a first for me. Up until this time, the prospect of finding an entire conch shell in its natural environment had always sparked me, but I was always sadly deflated when I dug the shell out of the sand and found it was a fragment.

In this instance, I expected to find the typical, broken fragments of a shell that had once been laced with beauty and symmetry, only to be ripped apart by the ocean waves, shifting sands, and storms at sea. I pulled on the corner of the shell, and it did not budge. There was hope; maybe this shell was still unscathed by the

> We'll be pounded in the crashing waves, but we'll also be changed.

sea's furor. It intrigued me enough to abandon my run and begin digging in the sand to find out.

After a few minutes of digging and pulling, there it was— amazing! I had finally done it! It took half a lifetime, but right there on the North Carolina Coast, I pulled an entire conch shell out of the deep sand. It was not without imperfection—there was a scar here, a disfigurement there—but for the most part, this conch shell was still fully formed, fully shaped and together, and glimmering with allurement and glamour!

I washed the shell off, took it home with me, and gave it to my youngest son, Baylon. He was so excited! It still sits on his bedroom dresser, proudly displayed. But there are parts of him that still think I bought it in a store. Nothing could be further from the truth. As rare as it is, it's the real thing, an uncommon find that rises above the ordinary. But the shell actually has more significance to me than a dresser ornament. It has significance to me because of what I heard an old seaman say one time.

> For our light and momentary struggles are achieving for us an eternal glory that far outweighs them all.
>
> 2 CORINTHIANS 4:17

Most of the shells you will find on the beach will be a broken fragment of what once was. But on a rare occasion, you'll find a shell that is still fully intact. When you do, you will have found something of great value. Don't overlook it! The shells that are broken are as such because they have resisted and fought the crash of the waves, the storms, the raging currents, and the shifting sands their entire existence.

The shells that remain fully intact are those that have discovered the great secret of submitting to the storms, the raging currents, the shifting sands, and the crash of the waves.

They have discovered that not resisting them is crucial to their formation and their beauty. They cannot circumvent the waves, so they roll with them. They accept them because they realize those crashing waves, storms, and shifting sands are necessary for making them what they are fully supposed to be. Such is life.

Since that moment, I've searched in hopes of finding a shell of such rarity. On that North Carolina beach, I found one, and the more I look at it, the more it tells that story. But I would add to the story that such is the faith-centered life.

The storms have a purpose for something that is far greater and far better than anything we can imagine.

2 Corinthians 4:17 (NIV) says, "For our light and momentary struggles are achieving for us an eternal glory that far outweighs them all." That verse is one of the only things that has ever made any sense of the suffering and anguish of this world, of this existence we call life. It's the only thing that has ever made sense of the mind-numbing, unexplainable affliction this life can assail us with at times. The storms, the shifting sands, the crashing waves, the raging currents—they have to be doing something. They must have a purpose for something that is far greater and far better than anything we can imagine. It's the only thing that makes sense of an incurable diagnosis or an untimely death or tragedy.

If we can learn not to resist or circumvent those crashing waves but to accept them and roll with them as part of the plan, something is forming that is so far beyond description that nothing else will compare to it. There has to be something awaiting such a magnanimous discovery that it will make sense of it all, and words won't be able to describe it. There has to be some treasure, some glory that lies deeper.

Submission and surrender don't mean giving up or giving in. They don't mean there's not a willful battle, or that we shouldn't hope for healing or deliverance. It simply means that regardless of the outcome, we realize, even if it's our own fault, God will redeem all things and purpose them for something of value. It means we know that it's doing something, even when it hurts and is not comfortable.

But it will require faith and trust. We'll be pounded in the crashing waves, but we'll also be changed. In the in-between moments of the mundane, we'll rest on the sand and enjoy the warmth and comfort of the sun. But we'll also be aware that we are waiting to be carried back out to sea for more.

Most people who learn to roll with life's storms and crashing waves are able to do so because they realize the storm is preparing them for their eternal home.

Do these types of shells exist in human form? They do. They are just as rare as the fully formed shells on the shore, but they exist. I've seen them; I've done life and faith with them and most commonly found them not on a seashore but sitting in a church pew. They are rare, but if you invest in a church body of people, you'll find them. When you find these rarities, you'll never be the same. But to find them, you must take the risk to ride upon the waves of relationships with others. You will have to show up, release yourself, and take down the walls around you. It could make you vulnerable, but it will make you better. This is not by accident. It is a divine appointment.

One more interesting thing about shells. Most seashells are nothing more than a temporary home for a wide variety of animals. The same is true in the Christian life. Most people who learn to roll with life's storms and crashing waves are able to do so because they realize the storm is preparing them for their eternal home. Everything here is temporary;

the glory in eternity that the current or next storm is producing will far surpass any experience on this earth.

The waves have a much different sound to me these days. The shells and the storms have a much different look. Each time I see one or hear a wave, I am reminded of the hope that something better is being built and that something better is always on the way.

> *Not only so, but we also glory in our sufferings, because we know that suffering produces perseverance; perseverance, character; and character, hope. And hope does not put us to shame, because God's love has been poured out into our hearts through the Holy Spirit, who has been given to us.*

Romans 5:3-5 (NIV)

In Conclusion

43

It Matters

If you are not familiar with the man named Job, you should become familiar with him. He was a man who was faithful and blameless. He was a righteous man who feared and walked with God. But he was also a man who suffered incredibly. His story is told in the Bible. He has an entire book dedicated to his experience with suffering. It is a great commentary and encouragement for any and all who go through suffering. If you live long enough, you will encounter a certain amount of suffering.

Do yourself a favor, and take the time to make a trip over to the Bible. Pick it up, open it midway to the book of Psalms, go back one book, and find Job. Read the book of Job from front to back. You will be better for it.

One of the best things about the Bible is that it is incredibly honest and real about the lives and names contained within its pages. Nothing is sugar-coated. We get the real people, along with their successes and mistakes. In Job we get the real story, and we see every part of his life experience. He is honest about his

> If you live long enough, you will encounter a certain amount of suffering.

struggles, and he holds nothing back. Some of those struggles are even with the God he serves.

In Job 19:23-24 (NLT), in the midst of his daily fight, we find Job expressing himself and his struggles. As he expresses his feelings, he writes, "Oh, that my words could be recorded. Oh, that they could be inscribed on a monument, carved with an iron chisel and filled with lead, engraved forever in the rock."

In expressing his thoughts and feelings, Job wanted his words of anguish to be etched in stone forever. He wanted his suffering to matter, as we all do. He wanted his torment to make sense, as we all do. He wanted his words to be saved so that other broken and suffering people could enter into his brokenness with him. He wanted his words to encourage and give hope to others through time, as do we all.

> Oh, that my words could be recorded. Oh, that they could be inscribed on a monument, carved with an iron chisel and filled with lead, engraved forever in the rock.
>
> JOB 19:23-24

If I had gone through the same experience as Job, I would want to know that my life and experiences mattered and counted for something. I would want my life to have some type of eternal value, especially the hard parts. I would want my experience to mean something and have eternal impact. I would want my words to endure. I would want something, anything, to matter beyond just my temporary experience.

Job likely thought his words would be forgotten. Perhaps at one time, he thought his life experiences would forever be filed away into that dreaded file folder called "Random and Meaningless." He likely had no idea his words would survive him, let alone have any eternal value. But that is exactly what happened. Everything Job experienced had significance and value beyond his awareness. The same is true with each of us. What happens to us matters.

Job's words were carved into something even better than a monument. His words were carved out with something more powerful than an iron chisel. Job's words were carved into the eternal, holy, powerful Word of God! They were preserved by the hand of God the Almighty, and they will be preserved forever. Job's words have

> When entrusted to God, every piece of our lives will have eternal significance.

served to encourage others for centuries, and they will continue to do so for eternity. He had no idea such a thing would happen. Nothing is random or meaningless with God. Nothing. When entrusted to Him, every piece of our lives will have eternal significance. Our lives matter.

Through the leading of God's Spirit, the Lord worked to bring about words that had eternal value through what Job thought were his random thoughts of anguish and brutal honesty. Think about it: from his suffering, honest hand, we get such timeless phrases as, "I came naked from my mother's womb, and I will be naked when I leave. The LORD gave me what I had, and the Lord has taken it away. Blessed be the name of the LORD!" Job 1:21 (NLT).

This phrase has been written into many hymns and worship songs, sung by millions throughout the ages. It has been shared in many times of grief or stated for comfort for grieving families at funerals.

Also from Job, we get what he thought was the soon-to-be-forgotten phrase, "But as for me, I know that my Redeemer lives, and he will stand upon the earth at last" Job 19:25 (NLT). It is this phrase, along with many others in Scripture, that a musician named Handel would take and incorporate into what we now know as the classic and timeless musical piece, "Handel's Messiah." It is that beautiful message about Christ the Redeemer that we hear each year through Handel's musical offering. Because of this musical offering inspired by Scripture itself, we hear beautiful reminders every Easter and Christmas season set to music that prompts us to be encouraged by the fact, "I know that my Redeemer lives!"

I'm sure Job would have never imagined his routine words would be put into a musical orchestration that would impact millions for years to come. I'm sure that Job had little idea that the Lord he served so faithfully, even in his suffering, would preserve his words and use them for something that millions would still read, sing, and be encouraged by to this day. His words were forever etched in the Rock of Ages, the Word of God, and they still have value today and through eternity. Your words matter.

> I came naked from my mother's womb, and I will be naked when I leave. The LORD gave me what I had, and the Lord has taken it away. Blessed be the name of the LORD!
>
> JOB 1:21

For Job, nothing was random about his anguish and turmoil. None of it was without purpose. His thoughts and contemplations were not haphazard. His life was not arbitrary. Every moment mattered, still matters today, and has been preserved for eternal impact. Every moment matters.

Of course, you're not Job. Your life is not Job's life, and honestly, you probably wouldn't want to live through what Job had to endure. But you have had struggles. As foreign as those struggles may seem to you, they matter.

You may have been caught in the fateful gutter of random and meaningless. You have likely wondered if anything you say or do matters. You have probably looked back and wondered if anyone will remember you or anything you ever did or said. You have probably wondered if anyone would even notice if you weren't here today. You have also likely had the desire that your words or part of your life could be recorded to encourage others or leave lessons to follow. You have likely wondered if anything from your life will be preserved or have eternal impact.

Perhaps, like Job, you have had friends who gave you bad advice or have even begun to abandon or turn on you. Perhaps you have had relationships turn sour. Perhaps you have experienced too much loss to think that anything good or eternal can come from it. But it all matters.

> But as for me, I know that my Redeemer lives, and he will stand upon the earth at last.
>
> JOB 19:25

Perhaps, for you, the God you thought you knew seems distant and silent. Perhaps the misery has overwhelmed you to the point of giving up. Maybe it's not even the suffering. Perhaps you can no longer take the boredom of your seemingly routine life where nothing seems to change.

Take a moment to fast forward to the end of Job's life. After an intense conversation with God, Job responded to God with these words in Job 42:5-6 (NLT): "I had only heard about you before, but now I have seen you with my own eyes. I take back everything I said, and I sit in dust and ashes to show my repentance."

Job 42:10 (NLT) tells us that the Lord blessed Job with "twice as much as before!" (v.10). We are told in the final verse that Job "died an old man who had lived a long, full life." In all his misery and anguish, Job did not lose sight of the greatness or faithfulness of his God. He came to realize that nothing about his life was random or without meaning. In his writings, carefully preserved for ages, we come to realize that everything about his life had eternal value. His life mattered.

For those who may feel like your life is random, boring, routine, or without value, take heart and listen to the life lessons from Job in the Bible. For those who may feel as though God has left you in the wind, disappeared, or seems silent and disinterested, take note of the God who walked and talked with Job through every part of his difficult routine and never left him. God walked with Job through the ups and downs.

Take note of the God who blessed Job with more than he could have ever imagined by the end of the story. Take note of the hard, the blessing, the suffering, and the beauty and lessons provided in them all.

Job came to realize that nothing about his life was random or without meaning. Every single second, minute, hour, day, month, and year of your life matters in the plan of God.

Look again at the God who took every single life experience of Job and carefully preserved them for eternity. Look again at the God who gave meaning to every ounce of Job's anguish. In the questions and doubts, even when Job could not see it, God was carefully etching every word and moment into His eternal story of redemption. Nothing was random; nothing was without meaning. Every part would matter later. Every part would matter for eternity.

Whatever random, boring routine you may be growing tired of, do not forget that God has you there for a purpose and a reason, even when you can't see it. Whatever suffering, anguish, and misery you may be experiencing, do not forget that God will not waste it. If you surrender to Him, God will use your story and experiences to encourage others, even long after you are gone. If you trust God, your life and experiences will not be forgotten. They will matter. Even if you live and die alone in Christ, God will bring your story gloriously into eternity. He will use your story to complete the ultimate plan of redemption. It matters.

Ultimately, if you surrender to Him and trust Him by faith, your life will have eternal impact. Every single second, minute, hour, day, month, and year of your life matters in the plan of God. You are not forgotten or abandoned, and your life has meaning, even the parts you would prefer to discard. As He did with Job, God is working in a way that is far beyond what you can see at the moment. Your life and moments, when surrendered to Him by faith, will be etched and woven into God's story of redemption for eternity.

> Through suffering, our bodies continue to share in the death of Jesus so that the life of Jesus may also be seen in our bodies.
>
> 2 CORINTHIANS 4:10

Remember the words of the Apostle Paul in 2 Corinthians 4:17-18 (NLT) that have been repeated throughout this book.

"For our present troubles are small and won't last very long. Yet they produce for us a glory that vastly outweighs them and will last forever! So we don't look at the troubles we can see now; rather, we fix our gaze on things that cannot be seen. For the things we see now will soon be gone, but the things we cannot see will last forever."

Job would agree with that truth. He came to live it, and he is living it for eternity. Even at the time of his own writings, the Apostle Paul could have had little idea that his words, written in letters to local churches, would become the sacred, hallowed, and eternal words of Scripture. Just before he wrote these words, the same Paul also recorded in 2 Corinthians 4:10 (NLT), "Through suffering, our bodies continue to share in the death of Jesus so that the life of Jesus may also be seen in our bodies."

That statement assures us that our current circumstances have eternal value. There is no amount of suffering, misery, loneliness, or routine in your life that God cannot redeem and use for eternity. Every single second of your life is pointing to something that is marvelously and gloriously more than you can see or imagine. Take nothing for granted. See the beauty of your routine. Know that your adversity is pointing to something greater. Remember that this is not your destination; this world is only the preparation for your destination. Your routine is beautiful and has purpose. Do not give up; do not lose heart. God is working your life into His eternal plan. Trust Him with your days and moments. It matters.

The little things are not little. The routine is far from boring. There are glorious adventures waiting for you every day in the valley and the ascent to the mountain. Your present circumstances are not the defining moment. They are pointing you to the defining moment. Hang on and walk by faith. Trust God to the end. It matters.

> Your adversity is pointing to something greater. Your present circumstances are not the defining moment. They are pointing you to the defining moment.

There is a difference between looking and seeing. It's not what you're looking at that matters; it's what you see. Once you learn to see the eternal purpose in every routine moment of your life, you will begin to experience the miracle of the mundane. Once you begin to experience that daily miracle, you will realize how much living God has for you on this earth and beyond.

Remember, Jesus said in John 10:10b (NIV), "I have come that they may have life, and have it to the full." When

> I have come that they may have life, and have it to the full.
>
> JOHN 10:10B

you trust Christ with your moments and days, your abundant life is not only coming, but it's here now. It will last forever, into eternity. This is the beautiful, hard, challenging, routine, mundane, miraculous, eternal life that God has planned for you. Wake up and live it! It matters.

44

The Water Sprinkler

My three sons stood by the water hose, filled with anticipation, trying their best to contain their excitement. It was as if they were about to come out of their shoes and float through the air. The smiles spread across their faces and the joy beaming in their hearts produced a sense of bliss and wonder in my own heart. I was smiling along with them, anticipating every moment.

We had just spent a long, hot summer afternoon together doing chores in the yard. Summer was in full force, blazing with its hot afternoon temperatures. The brown grass was longing for a respite from the hot and dry afternoons of another steamy, summer day in the south. Trees and bushes seemed to already be looking forward to the cool breezes of Fall. Shade was a valuable commodity on a day like this... unless of course, you had a water sprinkler.

Both myself and my three young boys were covered and dripping with sweat. Our fingertips were layered with the dirt from the flower beds. Constant was the swatting away of flies and gnats. The high humidity clipped the oxygen layer thinner than usual. As hard as each of these things were on this scorching day, their laborious nature seemed to make even sweeter the joyous anticipation of the water sprinkler.

Strangely, hard things always seem to make you more aware of the joy in the joyful things. Fittingly, we actually began to find the joy in the hard labor, all because we knew what was coming with the water sprinkler.

I had promised my boys, "If you work hard and complete all the work in the yard, we will get out the water sprinkler!" For them, that meant the joyous and refreshing run through the water streams jetting into the air. It would be the perfect response and compliment to a hot, summer day. When water parks and swimming pools are not readily available, the water sprinkler will do just fine.

The water sprinkler can change the atmosphere of an intensely hot day in just seconds. It can lift frowns and turn gritted teeth into animated smiles. It can make you forget about the sweltering conditions surrounding you. It can give you the gleeful escape to the extraordinary, right there in the ordinary of your own brown, dried-out, prickly front yard.

> We actually began to find the joy in the hard labor, all because we knew what was coming.

Carefully, I screwed the sprinkler onto the nozzle of the hose. There could be no leaks, no malfunctions. We had waited all day for this. I enthusiastically pulled the water hose and the sprinkler into the front yard of our home. My boys began to jump up and down and scream. My heart began to beat out of my chest, and my smile was as wide as the summer day is long. "Let's go! Let's go!", the boys began to scream. I responded, "Wait right there until I turn on the water!" Smiles were abounding everywhere in the driveway as we all waited with great expectation.

I turned the water spigot. Water began to shoot through the carefully designed holes of the water sprinkler. Into the sky the water streams flew! They seemed to go for miles into the hot, humid air. My boys jumped higher and higher, screaming louder with each jump! I quickly positioned myself on the other side of the sprinkler so that I could get the perfect picture. I was ready, they were ready. We had anticipated this joyful moment all day long!

I raised my hand and counted down, "Three, two, one... GO!" My three boys shot out of the driveway like a drag-race car on a drag strip! Screaming to the top of their longs, with joyful smiles on their faces, they shot through the streams of water!

I got the picture I wanted. I carefully put down my phone, and I jumped in with them. We laughed, we jumped, we screamed, we sang, we clapped and high-fived, we played, and we got soaked. Sure, the water did its own form of soaking. But what we were soaked with the most was joy and passion, and a sense of wonder. I promised myself that I would never forget that moment and what I felt, and I haven't.

I'll never forget the anticipation leading up to that moment. I'll never forget the excitement or the smiles. I'll never forget the sprint through the streams of water. I'll never forget the joyous screams, hugs, or the high-fives. I'll never forget the wonder a water sprinkler provided for us that day. It all seemed so simple, so ordinary, yet it was beautifully extraordinary.

I want to live my life this way. I want to greet each day and each moment with the same passion, force, and joy of running through a water sprinkler on a hot, summer day. I want to see each moment and each day for the gifts that they are, even the hard parts. I want my heart to beat out of my chest with the expectation that even in my most routine and ordinary moments of life, there is incredible potential for extraordinary to invade and take over.

I want to hope and believe that if I tie myself to the true Source of life (Jesus), God will send his life-giving streams through my veins and produce joyful and miraculous moments in the middle of my dry and mundane experiences.

I know there will be long, hot, and steamy seasons of my life. There will be moments when life's brokenness and humidity seem to be squeezing the oxygen out of my existence, making it hard to breathe and push forward. There will be moments when the sweat of trauma and suffering drip across my forehead with a ferocity that I can barely stand. There will be times when I seem to be doing nothing but swatting away the agitations of life as though they are gnats and flies. There will be times when life stains my heart and hands with the darkness of its harsh dirt. But each and every one of these things will only serve to increase my anticipation for the joyful things. Strangely, I may even learn to find joy in the hard things.

> I want to hold tightly to hope, even when it seems as if all hope is lost.

I want to look for the moments of refreshment. I want to be aware of the streams of joy shooting through the air, and accessible each day. I want to run to those streams as a kid runs through the sprinkler. I want to high-five, laugh, shout, smile, jump, and get soaked in the beauty of each second of life. I want to find those streams in the lowest of valleys, even in the valleys of death and mourning. I want to see those streams shooting through the highest mountain-tops of weddings, births, birthdays, game-days, and graduations. But I also want to recognize their joyous existence in my most boring and routine moments and days. They remind me that every single second is a gift, has purpose, and is doing something eternal.

I want to keep that look on my face...that look a child has when they're about to hit the streams of the water sprinkler. I want to have joy, even in adversity. I want to hold tightly to hope, even when it seems as if all hope is lost. I am promised by God that I will never find disappointment in this hope.

But I must also know that this unwavering, eternal hope can only be developed through the fiery trials of life. The sweltering heat of life's struggles will give me the great anticipation of the refreshment and joy coming from the streams of life waiting in the sprinkler of God's Spirit. Those streams of life will produce the exuberant sounds of hope in my life. That hope will keep me running with excitement toward each day. I want to run toward each moment with hope and joy, as a kid runs with force and joy through the water sprinkler.

> Even in my old age, let my passion for living each day grow stronger as I approach eternity.

My body may grow older and more exhausted with each passing year. I may lose a bit of that force and exuberance over time in my physical body. But let it never decrease in my spirit. Even in my fatigue and weariness, I want to run with this hope toward the streams of life. Even if I grow old enough that my pace slows to a walk, then let me walk with hope toward these streams. Even in my old age, let my passion for living each day grow stronger as I approach eternity. Even in the twilight years of my life, let this hope for the next day never die out, until I cross over into the streams of eternity.

This type of hope will give me the endurance to continue to live as though I'm running through the sprinkler. This hope will develop my character and help me be more aware of the joy in the joyful moments. It will make me more aware of the miraculous in the mundane. This hope will never disappoint me.

"We can rejoice, too, when we run into problems and trials, for we know that they help us develop endurance. And endurance develops strength of character, and character strengthens our confident hope of salvation. And this hope will not lead to disappointment. For we know how dearly God loves us, because he has given us the Holy Spirit to fill our hearts with his love." Romans 5:3-5 (NLT)

One day, I will come to the end. I don't know when that will be, only the Lord determines such things. But when it happens, all of the sweltering, dirt-filled labor will find me standing in the driveway of eternity. Maybe there will be a shout from my Heavenly Father, "Three, two, one...GO!" At that time, my brand-new body will shoot across Heaven's gates with the same force and passion that a kid runs through a water sprinkler on earth. I will run with joy and passion into the arms of the Savior who produced such life-giving streams for me all of my life—even in the hard parts.

In that moment, everything will tie together and make complete sense in the refreshment of eternity. There will be high-fives, shouts, singing, clapping, hugs, and most of all, we will be soaked in the glory of eternity, together forever. I promised myself I'll keep living with anticipation for that moment, and I haven't stopped yet. So stretch out the hose, turn on the water sprinkler, and let's run!

Made in the USA
Middletown, DE
08 September 2024

60240776R10177